Praise

"As children, none of us are a match for the world—make that the adults—around us. Lauren Rhoades delivers a clear lyrical account of that truth set in Nineties-era Denver suburbia. Bat-mitzvahed and then recast Catholic, she grew up a girl-sized, court-monitored rope in the post-divorce tug-of-war between her mother and father and stepmother. Due to Rhoades's sharp little eyes then and ample wisdom now, *Split the Baby* is engaging, heartbreaking, infuriating, and wry. This memoir makes the reader wonder how any of us arrive to adulthood in one piece. Rhoades can't say we do. All that's left is to behold our used parts and the ways they shape our lives and loves ever after. My heart grew a bit before Rhoades was through with me."

—Ellen Ann Fentress, author of *The Steps We Take: A Memoir of Southern Reckoning*

"There is a circularity to *Split the Baby: A Memoir in Pieces* as Rhoades explores the threads of a childhood bifurcated by divorce. In beautifully frank prose, she navigates her two homes and the two women she loved: the pain of a mother, a stepmother in competition. *Split the Baby* is an ethically generous memoir, told with compassion and grace, in which Rhoades shows us what it feels like to inhabit a body divided."

—Mary Miller, author of *Biloxi*

"Startlingly beautiful prose, effortlessly rendered, and never pretentious, *Split the Baby* is the most evocative and moving memoir I've ever read about childhood, marriage, and divorce. I cannot imagine a more therapeutic book for disintegrating families to read together. Lauren Rhoades has written a unique classic that will bring great solace to kids caught between bedrooms that often reflect the needs of the parent more than the child. Read this book and you will be giving it away as a gift forever."

—Lee Durkee, author of *Stalking Shakespeare* and *The Last Taxi Driver*

Split the Baby

Split the Baby

the

A Memoir in Pieces

Lauren Rhoades

Fort Smith, Arkansas

SPLIT THE BABY:
A MEMOIR IN PIECES

© 2025 by Lauren Rhoades
All rights reserved

Edited by Casie Dodd
Design & typography by Belle Point Press

Belle Point Press, LLC
Fort Smith, Arkansas
bellepointpress.com
editor@bellepointpress.com

Find Belle Point Press
on Facebook, Substack,
and Instagram (@bellepointpress)

Printed in the United States of America

29 28 27 26 25   1 2 3 4 5

Library of Congress Control Number: 2025935430

ISBN: 978-1-960215-36-9

STB / BPP46

For Sam.

A child which appears reasonably happy may actually be suffering horrors which it cannot or will not reveal. It lives in a sort of alien under-water world which we can only penetrate by memory or divination.

GEORGE ORWELL, "SUCH, SUCH WERE THE JOYS"

In a glass house...you cannot conceal anything without giving yourself away, except by hiding it under the ground. And then you cannot see it yourself, either.

ALICE MILLER, *THE DRAMA OF THE GIFTED CHILD*

Contents

A Note on the Parenting Diary   1
Split the Baby   3
Savior Complex   17
Parenting Diary: Pancake House   25
Daughter of the Commandment   27
Parenting Diary: Barnes & Noble   47
Little Brother, Little Sister   50
Parenting Diary: Winter Wonderland   66
Discernment   69
Parenting Diary: Fish Tank   86
Ghost Family   89
The Burning House   102
Parenting Diary: Pinewood Derby   121
Mirror, Mirror on the Wall   124
Children of Divorce   138
Epilogue   161
Bibliography   166
Acknowledgments   167

A Note on the Parenting Diary

Starting in August 1999, when I was ten and my brother Sam was seven, my mother began keeping what she called a "Parenting Diary," a composition notebook in which she recorded her interactions with Sam and me and with my father and stepmother. For some time, she had been distraught by the idea that she was "losing her kids," worried at a dramatic shift in our behavior and attitudes, including our refusal to see her during her scheduled custody time. She attributed this behavior to my father and my stepmother, Krystal. They were manipulating us, poisoning us against her, but how could she prove it? The notebook became a place for my mother to record her evidence.

My mother's entries were eventually included as part of a report she submitted to a psychologist and court-appointed special advocate whose responsibility was to "investigate, report, and make recommendations to the Court in the best interests of the minor children on issues relating to the parenting time schedule."

In 2019, twenty years after my mother started her parenting diary, my stepfather Cecil began sending me legal documents and records related to the parenting time disputes that took place throughout my childhood. Later, my mother reluctantly gave me the Parenting Diary itself, its cover worn and the pages loose but still intact.

"There's some painful stuff in here, things I was writing about you and Sam back when you didn't want to live with me," she said. "Are you sure you want it?"

I said I did. Both she and Cecil later told me that handing off these old papers was like lifting a physical burden from their shoulders.

I recognize and remember some of the incidents described in my mother's Parenting Diary. For example, I remember falling asleep in my bed with my coat still on, then waking up in my darkened bedroom and seeing my mother's worried face illuminated by the neon glow of my fish tank. I had done something bad, or something I had thought was good, but had turned out to be bad, and I just wanted to keep sleeping, to never wake up. But I couldn't remember what I had done, couldn't remember what came before. Fragments return to me in flashes. Reading my mother's words is like looking into a shattered mirror, seeing my reflection distorted into disturbing shapes. In this case, the distorted reflection is the truth.

What I'm trying to say is that in the Parenting Diary I am a stranger, but my mother is familiar. Her pain is now my pain. And her voice is what was missing from my memory.

Split the Baby

I never liked the Solomon story. You know the one. Two women come to the wise King Solomon, both claiming to be the mother of the same baby. King Solomon tells the women that since there's no way to know who the real mother is, he'll just cut the baby in half. One woman calmly accepts his proposal. The other falls to the floor, pleading that Solomon not harm the child, that he let the other woman raise the baby. This display of maternal selflessness is all the proof Solomon needs to identify the real mother. The baby is hers.

I first heard this story as a child in Hebrew school. As I sat on the carpeted floor that smelled like lemon cleaning solution, I wondered why the first woman was so ready to accept half a baby, or rather, a dead baby. Surely even a non-mother would prefer a live child to a dead one? And what if King Solomon's plan had backfired? Even his false proposal of infanticide seemed strange and cruel. The story nagged at me, with all its horrible possibilities, its myriad loopholes.

But I also couldn't help but dwell on the idea of cutting a baby in half. I was obsessed with the violent and graphic Hans Christian Andersen fairy tales, especially the one where the little girl begs an executioner to chop off her feet because they won't stop dancing. And in the Torah, God was always coming up with creative and horrific punishments—wiping out entire cities, killing off the Egyptians' first-born children, making the Jews wander in a desert for forty years, flooding the world. Slicing a baby down the middle—splitting its skull like two halves of a peach—didn't seem completely far-fetched. In my own gruesome version of the story, the baby survives, and each woman leaves the palace with half a baby cradled to her chest: one arm, one kicking leg, one watchful eyeball, one dimpled butt cheek. Each half baby would grow to be a half child, a half adult. Half a mouth, half a brain. Haunted by the desire to be whole.

As a child, I too felt split in half—pulled between the disparate worlds and needs of my divorced parents. Every child wants to be wanted, and I *was* wanted, but I did not understand the depth of that desire, its bitter vastness. This is what the wise king knew: that it is possible to become a fanatic of wanting, wanting what you cannot have, depriving others of what you yourself are deprived. That bitterness can taste sweet, like honey drizzled on unripe fruit. Nevertheless, the body remains indivisible—singular, whole, or nothing at all.

The *old house* is how everyone in my family refers to the house in Park Hill, the brick bungalow with the porch swing, linoleum kitchen floor, and the single stained-glass window by the fireplace. My parents purchased the house when they moved to Denver in the early 1980s after graduating from Washington State University with twin master's degrees in geology. For me, the story of the old house is my origin story, the place where my parents' marriage began and ended, the first place my brother and I called home.

Most of my memories in the old house involve my mother and Sam—who was born three years and three days after me—and later on my stepfather Cecil, who joined our family toward the end of the old house's tenure. After my father moved out—and before Cecil moved in—we'd take Sunday afternoon naps in my mother's waterbed, Sam on one side of our mother, me on the other. She'd always play the same cassette tape: thunderstorm sounds. We'd fall asleep to the low rumble of thunder and the patter of rain, even as sunshine streamed through the bedroom windows. My mother was tired in those days—

work-tired, single-mom-tired, depression-tired. In the waterbed, she could let herself float away for an hour or two. Years later, I would think of those thunderstorm tapes and yearn for rain, for an escape from Colorado's high desert plains and unrelenting blue skies.

My father is largely absent from my memories of the old house—he was often working late and taking night classes to get his MBA, but he also moved out when I was four, and childhood amnesia has erased most of those early imprints. The memories of him are from after the separation and divorce, when he'd come back to visit. He'd pick Sam and me up from the house and we'd go downtown to the Warwick Hotel where he was staying and order room service hamburgers. We'd jump on the springy hotel beds, dip cold french fries in ketchup, and look out the window at the skyscrapers. Then he'd take us back home, back up the smooth cement steps, back to our mother.

The only memory I have of both my parents together and married takes place in the bathroom of the old house. It was a small bathroom with a tiled floor, pedestal sink, and a tub where I once fell and split the soft skin under my chin. In the memory, the air is steamy because my father has just taken a shower. I am in the doorway, holding on to my mother's leg. My parents are talking, their voices drifting over me like clouds. I am listening quietly to their conversation, though I don't understand it. I am always listening.

My father is naked, his wet feet planted on the bathroom rug. He is a giant, his legs covered in soft hairs which are now wet and stuck to his skin. I am looking up at his naked body, which—in my memory—is clouded as if behind steamed glass. Suddenly, he looks down at me, startled by the intent curiosity of my gaze. "Get her out of here," he tells my mother, and I am shooed out of the room, the door closed. Memory over. For the first time, I am aware of a body's nakedness, aware of myself as a single body, a body existing apart from my parents' bodies. A calving glacier. A splitting.

And yet, in spite of this Freudian remnant, I was never curious about my mother and father's once romantic relationship, about the shattered past which had brought me and then my brother into existence. I only knew or cared that I was half my mother's and half my father's. Half Jewish. Half Catholic. My brother had my mother's looks; I had my father's. I might as well have been grown in a glass jar, as I believed so-called "test tube babies" were. In middle school, when a close friend began to lose her hair from the stress of her parents' divorce, I was strangely callous and unsympathetic. "What's the big deal?" I thought. "That your parents don't love each other? So what?"

I liked feeling jaded about the realities of love and marriage. In my high school journal, I wrote that my secret desire was to someday live in a cottage by the ocean with my "illegitimate daughter." It would be just the two of us, the ocean and the beachy dunes, a garden full of blue hydrangeas. Nobody else but us. This vision of my future daughter and me arrived fully formed, signaling a deeper, subconscious desire. My imagined cottage was a protective enchantment, an inner dwelling built perfectly to size like a hermit crab's shell. Inside my cottage, my future coexisted with my past. I was my own guardian, my own child.

I was seven when my mother sold the old house to a young couple who would go on to finish the basement and "pop the top," more than doubling the square footage. We moved to the suburbs for the same reason white, middle-class families have been moving out of the city and into the suburbs for generations: the schools. Our neighborhood was called Cherry Creek Vista, one pocket within a vast sprawl of monochromatic subdivisions, big box stores, and shiny-windowed office parks. In Cherry Creek Vista, we could no longer walk to the museum or the zoo or the public library. But we could drive anywhere on the widest, smoothest roads I'd ever seen.

The new house was twice the size of the old one, and it backed up to a public park and the neighborhood swimming pool. In the summer, we would wake early on Saturday mornings to the sound of swim meets: whistles and loudspeakers and cheers. My new school, Cottonwood Creek Elementary, was on the other side of the park. I remember seeing the school library for the first time, a sunny atrium filled with books and colorful beanbags. It was at least ten times larger than the cramped, one-room library at my old school.

Two months after we moved into the new house, my father and soon-to-be stepmother moved back to Denver from Houston. Or more specifically, they moved to Cherry Creek Vista, to a pale yellow house less than a mile away. This move was my family's watershed moment, a decision that irreversibly changed our lives.

"The current parenting dispute was precipitated by Mr. Rhoades's move back to Denver in June 1996," Dr. Katz, our family's forensic psychologist, wrote in the parenting time evaluation he conducted later that year. It had been three years since I had lived in the same state as my father. Now, he and my stepmother wanted fifty-fifty joint custody. As the psychologist noted, the disagreements and disappointments my parents faced "... existed prior to the move but were less overt ... when the parties lived in other states." Now, in close proximity to one another, my parents' simmering disputes turned volatile, and the deluge of lawyers, mediators, child psychologists, and court dates appeared only to fan their bitter flames. But no one stoked the flames more than my stepmother, Krystal.

Sometimes I forget that there was a time before Krystal existed in our lives. As one psychologist delicately put it, she was "an extremely outgoing, vivacious person whom others tend to either really like or really dislike." In other words, she made an impression. Decades later, when I find Dr. Katz on the internet and meet with him via Zoom, he confesses that he doesn't remember my brother or me. But despite having evaluated hundreds of families over his decades-long career, he remembers Krystal. Who was this woman who shouldered her way into our family?

Just a year earlier, Sam and I had spent a week with her and my father in their Houston condo. When we returned home, I reported matter-of-factly to my mother that Krystie—as her friends and family called her—had a lot of mirrors, and that she was often looking into those mirrors. Gilt framed mirrors on the walls, mirrors on the antique vanities, full-length mirrors in the bedrooms. She was a woman who admired her own reflection, who needed to be admired by the people around her. Krystal was a former prom queen, a beauty pageant winner, the captain of her high school's cheerleading squad. She could knot a maraschino cherry stem in her mouth in under a minute. She liked to say, without a trace of irony, that "blondes have more fun," before flashing a bright white smile and brushing back her highlighted hair. She wore makeup and expensive jewelry. She thought drinking beer was unladylike. She loved that her coworkers called her "Barbie."

In trying to make sense of this woman, I had already begun to compare and contrast her with the most important woman in my life: my mother. Krystie liked gold, while Mom liked silver and turquoise. Krystie's hair was thin and light and straight, while Mom's was thick and dark and curly. Krystie owned silk nightgowns and floral kimonos, while Mom slept in an old, baggy T-shirt. My mother, whose nails were always unpainted and uneven, called Krystal's long acrylic nails "red daggers." She referred to Krystal as "the live-in" with such vehemence that I knew I should hate my soon-to-be stepmother, too. And though Krystal did frighten me, I was also involuntarily drawn to her, fascinated by her luminous smile, her jewelry box and makeup bag, her curling iron and collection of lotions and floral perfumes.

That winter, as lawyers haggled over drop-off times and divvied up holidays and school breaks, my father and Krystal married in the living room of the yellow house. My stepmother wore a maroon dress, her highlighted blonde hair teased, back-combed, and hair-sprayed into a puffy cloud. I wore a matching maroon velvet dress with itchy wool tights and Sam wore a little V-neck sweater and slacks, and after the ceremony, we played upstairs with the neighbor kids whose parents were drinking champagne in the kitchen. It had been six months since my father and Krystal had moved into their new house, and already she knew everyone on the block, had invited everyone in the vicinity to witness her newfound marital bliss. Like a self-appointed queen bee, she had already begun to orchestrate her world so that she was at the center, while the rest of us hovered around her, dutifully playing our parts.

Krystal made the yellow house her own: she painted all the bedrooms, furnished every room with mahogany antiques, hung oil paintings and crucifixes and mirrors on the walls. She made Sam and me her own, too, by picking out our clothes and decorating our rooms. Perhaps that's why she chose my father in the first place. She thought he would give her what she wanted: a beautiful house, two children, a picture-perfect life.

In just a few months, Sam and I had gone from sharing a bedroom to having two bedrooms apiece. Unlike the children in fairy tales, our lives had not been diminished by the arrival of our stepmother, but divided and then multiplied. We had not been banished to the cellar or the forest. Instead, we were now in the land of cul-de-sacs and castles, with two second-story bedrooms, two wardrobes, two lives.

From the beginning, Krystal wanted us—her stepchildren—in a way that confounded me. Most stepparents have a benign tolerance for their stepchildren. A tolerance that might lead to acceptance and eventually grow into love. The worst stepparents are, of course, the evil stepmothers in fairy tales, the ones with ulterior motives, who make their stepchildren sift through ashes, or banish them, or gift them poison apples. Sam and I already understood the concept of a stepparent: we had Cecil. I knew that Cecil cared for us, and even loved us. He cooked us dinner, dropped us off at soccer practice, washed our laundry, read bedtime stories to us in a monotone voice. But I also was vaguely aware that he did these things because of our mother. He loved us because he loved our mother. Without her, there would be no Cecil.

Krystal, however, came into our lives with a strange intensity and passion, a love that hinged on possession. I had no precedent, no framework to help me understand our relationship. In his observations of our family, even Dr. Katz noticed how Krystal "took over and attempted to control how the children played," and how confused Sam and I became, responding with "increased agitation, refusal to cooperate, and shutting down."

I soon began to confuse my stepmother's intensity for love. She raked her long, red nails against our skin in a way that raised goosebumps, kissed us on the mouth, took us to Christmas gatherings with her family. She taught me the words to the "Hail Mary" and the "Our Father" and gave me a slender gold ring inlaid with tiny rubies and diamonds, an enchanting little talisman that I wore to elementary school on my middle finger. My father was certainly under her spell. He was going to Catholic mass regularly for the first time since graduating from a Catholic high school. He listened to the music she liked, paid for the vacations she wanted to go on, and fought for his children the way she wanted him to, with no holds barred. Dr. Katz reported that my father "had a difficult time providing his own clear self-definition," that first he had allowed my mother to define who he was. Now he was allowing his new wife to do the same.

Sam and I adjusted, grew up the dual citizens of these two warring fiefdoms. We were fluent in the customs and rituals of both places. At Dad's, we held hands and prayed before we ate: "Bless us, O Lord, and these thy gifts, which we are about to receive through thy bounty, through Christ our Lord." At Mom's we observed Shabbat. Sam and I would fight over who got to strike the match and light the candles, and then we all touched our pinkies to the challah as we sang "*hamotzi lechem min haaretz*, we give thanks to God for bread . . ." At Dad's we were taught to answer the phone with "Rhoades' residence," even after we got caller ID and knew when our friends were calling. The TV there was kept in a locked box and video games were not permitted. Mom, on the other hand, never hesitated to give in to our requests. She and Cecil bought us a golden retriever puppy and a Nintendo 64. On weekends, we could watch cartoons while eating cereal on the couch, something we would never dream of doing on Krystal's white antique furniture.

My allegiances were constantly shifting between parents; my actions often seemed like a series of betrayals. I became a double agent, a diplomat, a secret keeper, a liar by omission and commission. The first real betrayal took place when I was eight years old and stole a piece of crumpled paper out of my mother's trash can. At the time, I was obsessed with *Harriet the Spy* and had taken to hiding and watching members of my family, making notes about their behavior in my notebook. Surveillance, I quickly learned, is a mostly dull job, and so I looked to other forms of snooping.

The crumpled paper I found was a letter my mother had drafted to her lawyer, Mary Davis. A lawyer, I vaguely understood, was someone who went to battle for you. These battles happened in court, which was a place with wood paneling, where a judge in a black robe made decisions about your life, much like King Solomon. My parents' lawyers existed for me as disembodied names overheard in adult conversations—Mary Davis, Lucy Benson. I had never seen them, never heard their voices, and yet they took on mythic proportions in my imagination. Mary and Lucy wore power suits with padded shoulders and high heels; they yelled at each other about who was best—mother or father. I was afraid of them, of how deeply my parents trusted them, of the enormous power they seemed to wield over our lives. In the letter, my mother's words were angry and unfamiliar. I read phrases like "Mary, you wouldn't believe ... ," and "in violation of the parenting agreement." My father's name was in it, as was Krystal's. "The children ..." I read over and over. "The children ..."

Suddenly it became clear what I had to do. Like a good spy, I would show the letter to my father and stepmother. I smoothed the crumpled paper, folded it, and hid it in my backpack, waited a few days until I knew I would see them. Then I proudly pulled the letter out and showed it to them as if it were a school project.

"Look," I said. "Look what I found."

My father and stepmother enjoyed the letter; they scoffed and snorted while reading it. Clearly, they understood more than I had. Krystal suggested that my father call Lucy and tell her what "the ferret" was up to. They told me what a good girl I was for helping them. I had wanted to help them, but I wondered now if helping them meant hurting Mom. I felt acutely, suddenly sad. I was imagining my mother in our house—"your other house," as Dad and Krystal called it—without us, and the image of her overwhelmed me. Mom was alone. Yes, she had Cecil, but I knew she missed her children, the ones who once curled around her body in the waterbed, listening to the sounds of thunderstorms. I regretted what I had done and resolved never to tell her, my treachery compounded by my absence. As far as I know, she never learned about my spying. If she did, she never told me.

After that, I would often wonder what my parents were doing when we were not there. A strange thing, to only know half someone's life. To leave your bedroom empty half the time. I would avoid going by the other parents' house when it was not their assigned day. When it was unavoidable, like if I forgot a school book, seeing them felt somehow like cheating, or awkward, like saying goodbye to someone, and then crossing paths an hour later. I could never give enough of myself, could never properly dole out my affections in a way that felt equitable.

For many years, I thought that something was wrong with me. Without clearly understanding what it was, I thought I might have multiple personality disorder. What else could explain why I behaved so differently at each house? Even my best friend Sarah said she could tell whose house I was at depending on the way I acted at school, what clothes I wore. Was I carefree and goofy? Wearing my slim-cut bell-bottom jeans? Must be at Mom's. Was I serious and quick-tempered, wearing turtleneck sweaters? It must have been Dad's weekend.

A few months away from my high school graduation, I pondered what my life would look like in college and beyond. I wrote in my journal, "What kind of person will I be? I feel like two people now. When I have a husband and children, will I act differently at one house? Will my kids like one grandma better than the other? Will I be happy? Will I pursue what I want?"

I could not imagine what my life would look like as a single, undivided human. Who would I be? I had lived two half-lives for so long. I had two religions, two senses of humor, two sets of clothes. Would I settle somewhere in the middle? I understood intuitively that things could not keep careening forward like this, with me hovering between the poles of mother and stepmother. In the unfathomable future, the hypothetical grandfathers didn't worry me, but the grandmothers did.

In *The Uses of Enchantment*, psychoanalyst Bruno Bettelheim argues that fairy tale evil stepmothers serve as emotional scapegoats for a child's feelings of anger and animosity toward their own mother. By placing blame on the stepmother instead of the mother, "the fairy tale suggests how the child may manage the contradictory feelings which would otherwise overwhelm him." As a child, I was often overwhelmed by contradictory feelings, yet I was unable to locate an emotional scapegoat. When Dr. Katz asked me what it was like to go back and forth between houses, I said I "kind of" missed whatever family I was not with, but that I "tried not to think about it that much." I was obsessed with fairness, with making sure each house had its equal share of me.

Half the time, I saw my mother as she appeared before me. My mother, with her high cheekbones and round face framed by thick, dark hair, her silly dance moves, and her heightened sensitivity. I saw myself—my own silliness and sensitivity—reflected in her. The other half of the time, I saw my mother filtered through the eyes of my stepmother—my mother was "the ferret," "the birth mother," "the poison pen." Which version was true? And which version of myself was real? I was squinting at my reflection, at my stepmother, at my mother, trying to figure out which one of us was standing in front of a fun-house mirror.

Bettelheim says that similarly, a child may split themselves in two, unwilling to recognize their bad behavior as their own. "As the parent in the fairy tale becomes separated into two figures, representative of the opposite feelings of loving and rejecting, so the child externalizes and projects onto a 'somebody' all the bad things which are too scary to be recognized as part of oneself." This explains how I could love my mother and spy on her. I was simply scared of myself, of my warring impulses. Even now, I do things in my dreams which appall me when I awaken. I cheat on my husband, I lie to my best friend, I scream in Krystal's face, and then grab onto her arm, which falls off in my hands. I am still scared of the half that is hidden, and of what that half might do.

I was in my early twenties when I saw my parents' wedding photos for the first time. My grandmother had kept them in a box, mixed in with other family photos. Nearly fifteen years had passed since my father married my stepmother in the living room. I hadn't seen Krystal since I was nineteen, shortly before my father told me they were getting a divorce.

Surreal then to be sitting at my grandmother's glass-topped kitchen table, to see photographic evidence that my parents had once held each other's hands, fed each other cake, smiled lovingly into each other's faces. The baby's breath in my mother's hair, her off-the-shoulder gown. My father's hay-colored mustache, his tuxedo and thick-rimmed glasses. I felt slightly ill looking at them, at their gross display of togetherness, which I had known only for the briefest of moments. Any memories I had of their love had long been cannibalized by my child brain. I had almost forgotten that Sam and I were products of this pair, the union of two incompatible people.

When I think about the Solomon story now, I think of my mother and stepmother, and their bitter showdowns over who was the real mother and who was the impostor. Perhaps, as one psychologist suggested, Krystal was unaware of the "underlying competitiveness, hostility, and interpersonal difficulties in the family situation." Or maybe, she thrived on competition, on the thrill of a fight, even as my mother retreated like a wounded gazelle.

The Solomon story played out over and over again, in the absence of any judge or jury. Being in the same space as my mother and stepmother meant breathing with a sandbag on my chest. Time would slow and the mental calculations would begin—who would I sit next to? How long would I speak with each parent? Would I wave goodbye or cross the room to give a hug? Each word, each gesture became freighted with meaning as the two versions of myself played a violent game of tug-of-war inside my gut. Though it pains me now to admit it, if pressed into choosing a side, I would most often choose Krystal. It was easier that way. My mom loved me unconditionally, whereas Krystal had the power to make my life a living hell.

I wouldn't have blamed my mother if in the interest of self-preservation, she had contemplated the possibility of giving me up, letting my stepmother have me, if that's what I wanted. But my mother never relinquished me. She clung tightly to the half that was hers, even as I pushed her away.

In the end, Krystal left without saying goodbye, without a fight, or a final parting word—to me at least. I was nineteen, a sophomore in college, when my father told me that she was gone.

"She has this switch," he said, "and once you flip it off, you can't flip it back on."

He explained how Krystal had come to believe I was a spy for my mother, even though I was living in a dorm an hour away. I had sensed that Krystal had been pulling away from me ever since I left for college—it had been months since we had spoken—but now it seemed as though my father was talking about a stranger. After all, it was my mother I had spied on, not my stepmother.

Had Krystal only wanted me as her daughter so that my mother could not have me? Perhaps the simplest explanation was the right one: Krystal was jealous of Mom. When she knew she couldn't have all of me, she chose . . . nothing.

I was left to ponder what this meant now for my life, my future. I was alone, standing on the cold stone floor of the palace, facing the judgment of my past. Maybe I could become whole again. My ears, my eyes, my brain, my body—unsplit.

Savior Complex

I learn the word "crucifix" when my father tells a funny story—or less a story, and more a scrap of dialogue—about the woman he overheard at the jewelry store. Over time, this scrap will be rubbed shiny smooth with each retelling, like the nickel a magician pulls from behind your ear—delightful, but only the first time. This is how it goes:

"I'd like to buy a gold cross necklace," the woman at the jewelry store says.

"Of course," says the jeweler. He reaches inside the glass case and pulls out a display of various gold crosses, large and small. Some with diamonds on them, some plain. The woman inspects them, dissatisfied.

Finally, she asks: "Do you have any crosses with the little man on them?"

My father pauses here, then bursts out laughing. His laugh is like a small explosion: a rush of air, high pitched, then a downward cadence, like an arpeggio. His blue eyes crinkle, his mustache dances. At seven years old, I crave the sound of his laugh, his attention. For a few years, starting not long after Sam was born, my father lived in another house, then another state. He was a voice on the phone, a weekend visitor. In other words, he was once scarce, and perhaps this scarcity is what has made him even more precious to me.

I hang on his words, I mirror his laugh with my own—*haha!*—even though I do not understand the funny part of the woman's question. Like her, I have also noticed that some crosses have a little man on them. Some don't. I am picturing my father in the jewelry store, listening with a sly smile on his face, recording the conversation for later. Was he there to buy something for my stepmother? I remember the time he took Sam and me with him to buy Krystal an amethyst tennis bracelet, and I learned that the bracelet had nothing to do with the sport. She's wearing it now, the purple gems glinting when she moves her wrist.

"Krystie's cross has a little man on it," Sam says, pointing to our stepmother's neck, where a slender gold cross dangles from a thin gold chain.

"That's right," she says, leaning closer so we can see it. "It's not just any man. Do you know who that is on the cross?"

"Jesus," I say, before Sam can beat me to it. I look to my father, who nods his approval. The gold Jesus is a miniature of the one that hangs on the wall near the front door, which is nowhere near as big as the one that hangs behind the altar at St. Thomas More Church. Seeing Jesus's figure makes me woozy—ribs straining against his skin, blood oozing from his side, hip bones sharp as knives. My eyes sweep over his every bone, ligament, stringy muscle. "Gruesome" is the word I've heard my mother use when she talks about the Catholic Church.

"Jesus is hanging on the cross, which means that this cross is a *crucifix*," my father says. "Because Jesus was *crucified* on the cross."

"And they put nails through his hands?" Sam asks, eagerly.

"Through his hands *and* his feet. He died for our sins," my stepmother says. She rubs the crucifix between her forefinger and thumb, manicured nails glinting, before tucking it inside her sweater.

On my own neck hangs a gold necklace, a Star of David, which my mother gave me, only me. She doesn't wear one, and Sam doesn't either, I guess because he's a boy. My stepfather Cecil doesn't wear one, but that's because he isn't Jewish, though he goes to synagogue with us and doesn't care about celebrating Christmas.

I like wearing the necklace because it shows I am different than most of my other classmates, that I am special in some way, like when I get to miss school for the High Holidays, or when my friends find out that I celebrate Christmas *and* Hanukkah. There are other Jewish kids in second grade at Cottonwood Creek Elementary. We blend in with our mostly white Christian classmates, but we are different from them in subtle ways, different enough that we are the ones chosen to spin around like dreidels during the one Hanukkah song in the school's holiday musical.

Identity is a concept that I don't understand yet. My identity is just a collection of traits, a bingo card of belonging and not belonging. I am a girl. A blonde, blue-eyed girl. A blonde, blue-eyed Jewish girl. A blonde, blue-eyed Jewish girl who celebrates Christmas. I pick up the pieces of myself that I have been given and put them together, puzzling out what they mean. Soon, I will begin to see the contradictions inherent in my *self*. I will learn to camouflage and contort, to become a mirror, reflecting back the girl that others think they want to see. But for now, I am wholly me. This is who I am.

I am wearing the Star of David necklace when Dr. Katz conducts his home visits and interviews that will eventually help determine my parents' custody time. He is dark-haired and middle-aged, with wire-rimmed glasses and a kind smile. He is unlike any adult I have ever met, in that he listens more than he talks, sitting cross-legged on the carpet while he asks me questions. He watches everything that I do, which is both thrilling and disconcerting. I can't decide whether to perform and act silly, or to shrink down inside myself. Instead, I swing between these extremes like a pendulum.

Dr. Katz is observing us and talking to us in order to determine how much time Sam and I should spend at our father's house. My father wants us at his house half the time, and my mother doesn't want to give us up, plus she's mad that he and Krystal have been taking us to church even though their divorce agreement says that the children would be raised Jewish. In his report, Dr. Katz writes that my mother is concerned by the things Sam and I have been saying, things that, in her opinion, Jewish kids shouldn't say. Recently, Sam came home and asked why we don't believe in the baby Jesus. "It's not that we don't believe that Jesus ever existed, it's just that we don't believe that Jesus was a messiah," my mother answered, which left us all feeling confused. My father tells Dr. Katz that he wants his children to receive "exposure" to Catholicism, as though we are fragile seedlings that need to be moved from the greenhouse to the outdoors, hardened off. He complains that his ex-wife coddles the children; she lacks discipline. "Sometimes," he says, "you need to bring the hammer down."

Dr. Katz talks to me about Hebrew school. He asks me about my Star of David necklace, and I tell him that my mother got it for me two weeks ago. He scribbles a little note on his yellow legal pad. He asks me about my religion, and I begin to withdraw. Religion is bigger than me, bigger than St. Thomas More Church and Temple Sinai, bigger than my mother and father, my stepmother and stepfather, bigger than Friday nights and Sunday mornings. It's hard to keep straight the things I am supposed to believe, like who is or isn't the messiah, or what *messiah* even means. But religion is small too. As small as the symbol that hangs around a neck. My stepmother and my father wear crucifixes. I wear a Star of David.

In his report, Dr. Katz records what I say:

> "My mom is Jewish. I celebrate Christmas. I go to Dad's house every Christmas." [Lauren] indicated that her mother recently stopped letting her go to church anymore with her father. When asked how she felt about this, she said, "I really don't think I should go to church, because I'm not Catholic."

Reading the report as an adult, I wonder if the necklace was my mother's attempt to claim me. *Look*, she was saying, *this is my daughter. She may look like her father, but she is mine. She is Jewish.* The Star of David on my neck was like the identification sewn into the inside of a child's jacket. *If lost, call this number, find this address.* It was a visible reminder to my father, my stepmother, and to Dr. Katz that I belonged to her. But most of all, it was a reminder to me, her oldest child.

Did she intuit that I would be the child most likely to drift away from her, unmoored? My brother, who Dr. Katz described as "an energetic, affectionate boy, with few apparent problems," clung tightly to our mother, couldn't fall asleep unless she was lying on the floor beside his bed, cried easily when his feelings were hurt. His face was the spitting image of my mother's face when she was his age. Even his name, Samuel, comes straight from the Hebrew Bible. Samuel, a prophet, a ruler of Israel. My father's name is equally biblical, plucked straight from the New Testament: Matthew. A solid, sturdy Christian name. The apostle whose name I heard echoed in mass. *This is the Gospel according to Matthew....* But who is Lauren? Related to the laurel tree? The name of a famous actress? Maybe my roots have always been shallow, vulnerable to disturbances in the soil. Maybe this is why it has always been easy for me to pick up and go, to say goodbye without looking back. Or maybe that is another myth I tell myself.

Dr. Katz's "Parenting Time Evaluation" reads like a prophecy that has already come to pass. The star on my neck would offer me scant protection against the onslaught of religious propaganda we would receive at our father's house. Dr. Katz records this moment during his visit to Krystal and my father's house:

> Toward the end of the home visit, Sam asked that his father or Krystal bring down a crucifix. Sam wanted to show it to the evaluator. Krystal asked Sam what it said, and Sam didn't know what Krystal was talking about. Krystal had wanted him to say "King of the Jews." Sam talked about what a terrible way it was to die. Krystal asked the names of Jesus's mother and father, and Sam said, "Mary and David." Matthew explained that it was Joseph. Matthew then went into some other Bible stories the family had been talking about, asking Sam who the good

and bad guys were, and Sam said that the Philistines were the bad guys. Lauren said that Jesus did look like he was suffering.

Dr. Katz, himself a Jew, does not call my stepmother an anti-Semite. He tiptoes around the word, worried, perhaps, about appearing biased. He leans instead on observations: Krystal's exaggerated ignorance, her dismissal of Jewish tradition and belief. I can't help but wonder if the hairs on the back of his neck raised as the crucifix came off the wall. How did he feel when Krystal referred to Jesus as the King of the Jews in his presence? Did his body tell him that this was an act of hostility? Friends of mine would later tell me that my stepmother scared them. *Something about her eyes.* Perhaps she scared Dr. Katz, too. But his report is an exercise in restraint. He delicately proposes that my father and stepmother "might benefit from a meeting with the rabbi at Temple Sinai."

> The evaluator pointed out that one of the problems was that for the Jewish people, Jesus was not a king. Krystal indicated that she was finding it really hard to know what to do because she wasn't Jewish, and didn't know what it meant to be Jewish. She said it takes a concerted effort on her part to leave out Christianity in her interactions with the children.

To Dr. Katz, my stepmother claims she is Christian to her core, so Christian, in fact, that she couldn't possibly understand any other way to move through the world. She and my father "lived their lives in a Catholic context." The elephant in the room, of course, was us—my brother and me. Living proof that my father had chosen to live outside the Catholic context for years.

Now, decades later, I yearn for an unfiltered version of the parenting report in which "the evaluator" tells us what he is really thinking. One where the "I" isn't conspicuously missing. In this version, Dr. Katz is my golem, my Jewish monster and superhero, whose divine and single purpose is to save Sam and me from persecution. In this version he extracts us from the building before the spark is struck, defuses what he predicts will be a "ticking time bomb." But Dr. Katz was not a golem, just a man getting paid to do a job. He wasn't there to act, but to observe. And what would it mean to be saved, anyways? I don't believe in being saved anymore.

I don't think Dr. Katz would be surprised to learn that the Christian indoctrination continued, steadily unraveling the bond between mother and daughter. I don't think he would even be surprised to learn that for years afterward, Krystal would refer to him as "that *hebe* doctor." Three years after Dr. Katz submitted his reports, another family psychologist would sum up the continued custody battles as "a fight for the hearts and souls of the minor children." He would lament that "the children have not had (and developmentally would not be expected to have) the strength to resist the seductiveness of Mr. and Ms. Rhoades 'teaching of Christianity' to them."

In 2019, I began writing about my childhood and remembered the child psychologists and their curious, muted presence. I also remembered my parents referring often to the "Parenting Time Evaluation," though I had never seen the document.

"What happened to those reports?" I asked my mother.

"Oh god, you don't want to read those," she said. I assured her that I did. Dutifully, my stepfather went to the basement and rummaged through old boxes to find them. My mother had wanted to throw them away years ago—they were reminders of unhappy times—but Cecil had saved them. Somehow, they had survived three moves. ("I wasn't sure why I saved them, but I did," he would later tell me.) He brought the reports to his office, scanned them, and emailed them to me. On the day after my thirtieth birthday, I opened the email while I was still at work, read the reports straight through, and then lay on the floor and cried.

Now as I descend into the deep well of memory, these reports are the wobbly rope ladders that I cling to. When I begin to doubt myself, to question who I was then and who I am now, when I find myself inside the cave, I reach for the ladder: fifty-five single-spaced, witness-bearing pages. Someone else listened to me and heard what I wasn't able to say. Someone else saw me, not as a daughter or a stepdaughter, but as a child, suspended between worlds, looking for a savior. In finding her, I find myself.

Parenting Diary: Pancake House

September 27, 2000—Sent a letter to Matt regarding Yom Kippur and asking him to drop off the children at my house at 9 a.m. on October 9 because we were going to early services.

October 2, 2000—Received a long letter from Matt, faxed to my office, with some strange allegations. At the end of the letter he wrote "Also, please note that since you are keeping Lauren and Sam out of school on Monday, October 9, I will drop the children off at your house at 10 a.m. just as we did during the summer months."

October 9, 2000—The kids were dropped off at 10:15 a.m. and Krystal had taken them to The Pancake House for a big breakfast before Yom Kippur services. We missed the 9 a.m. services we were going to go to.

Inside the Pancake House, the walls are painted lingonberry blue. The smell of bacon grease and sugared apples makes mouths water, makes empty stomachs groan with longing. Pancakes are all we want. Only pancakes day and night, for a whole week, a whole month, an eternity. We are soothed by the clatter of dishes, the din of conversation, the circular motion of the busboy's rag as he clears another table of syrupy debris. A waiter walks by holding a giant Dutch Baby Pancake topped with powdered sugar for a table to share. We all pause to coo and stare at it, hungrily, as if it were a real baby on a plate, its pale, hot flesh steaming in the morning light.

We order glasses of orange juice, steaming cups of coffee. We fiddle with the packets of sugar, the little carafes of syrups, our waiting filled with a sense of purpose. Homework will be done. Parents won't fight. Sins will be absolved. Pancakes loaded with chocolate chips, studded with blueberries, stuffed with coconut, with pineapple, with bacon, topped with whipped butter that melts in rivulets, pooling in the crevices of the warm, fluffy, cooked-to-perfection batter. We jab forkfuls of sticky softness into our mouths, chew on sausage and bacon until our jaws hurt from the effort. Until we feel sick.

In the Pancake House, time ceases to exist. Time never existed in the first place. In the Pancake House, God never created heaven nor earth, nor the fish of the sea, nor the creatures of the land, nor darkness, nor light. In the Pancake House there is no dawn nor dusk, no such thing as *Yom Kippur*, the Day of Atonement. God only created pancakes.

Polish that off, my stepmother says. *One more bite. There you go.* She wants us to be full on this day of emptiness, repentance. She wants us to forget where and who we came from. Under her watchful eye, we stuff ourselves with the bounty before us like the Israelites who, believing themselves to be forsaken, shaped a golden calf and worshipped at its hooves. We emerge into the morning light, fattened and blinking. Only then do we remember our mother, her hunger.

Daughter of the Commandment

The first thing I notice about Shayna is her Jewishness, which radiates about her like a golden aura. She is short and slight and carries herself with the posture of a dancer, long hair stretching down her back in loose waves. She smiles often: at me, at our mothers—who have arranged this meeting—and at Cherie, who will be leading our first bat mitzvah teachings. I warm to Shayna instantly, even though I am usually wary of new people, shy and self-conscious, anxious about being liked. I learn that she is a singer, and that she sings opera. I tell her that I play piano and the cello in my school orchestra. We are twelve, and will be turning thirteen within months of one another. We attend different middle schools, but they both feed into the same high school. Already, I want to be her friend.

We are in Cherie's house outside of Denver, in the Foothills. The day is blustery and cold. A rare cloudy day in Colorado. Shayna's mother, Barbara, and my mother met in a *havurah* group, discovered that they both have daughters who were soon to be bat mitzvah age. Cherie is Barbara's friend, a Jewish Renewal educator, storyteller, and writer. We fold our coats over a chair by the door and sit at her kitchen table. The house is cozy with wood beams, tapestries, books, and the warm, smoky smell of incense. Cherie has brewed tea, and we hold the cups ceremonially in our hands, as though at any moment we might be asked to peer into the tea leaves and see what the future holds.

I know there is no single way to look or be Jewish, even though my stepmother believes that Jews wear their identities like a badge. "Trees," she calls us, a made-up term she uses to be discreet. *Trees* because we stand out, like a twisted cottonwood surrounded by prairie. *Trees*, like what Jesus was crucified on. *They're trees*, she might say about the women in this room, and they would instantly be reduced to caricatures—miserly, frumpy, frizzy, loud. I try my hardest to be the prairie and not the tree. I try to blend in, sending my roots deeper and deeper underground.

And yet, in this room of Jewish women, surrounded by the symbols of our religion—mezuzah, candlesticks, Kiddush cup—I sense that I am deficient. They talk easily with one another, finding refuge in each other's presence. I feel conspicuous with my blonde hair and light eyes, features that easily allow me to pass for a *goy* whenever I choose, but more than that, I'm aware of some invisible lack. I don't *feel* Jewish. Around this table vibrates a low, barely audible frequency that speaks to a common ancestral link. Something invisible—a knowing or a belonging—connects the women here. Shayna hums inside this frequency; she embodies her Jewishness, harmonizes with it. I, on the other hand, am an out-of-tune instrument, always a half note sharp or flat.

"A bat mitzvah is like a door at the end of a steep pathway," says Cherie, beginning our first lesson. She speaks slowly, like she's carving each word out of stone. A large silver *hamsa* dangles from a slender chain around her neck. "To get there, you must walk step by step, one foot in front of the other. With each step, you get a little stronger, a little wiser, a little older. By the time you reach that door, you are ready to enter womanhood, to take your place in the Jewish community. Do you know what a *mitzvah* is?"

"A commandment," Shayna answers brightly.

"That's right," Cherie says. "There are 613 of them in the Torah! And what about *bat mitzvah*? What does that mean?"

I am silent, unsure. I am grateful when Shayna speaks again.

"It means 'daughter of the commandment.' *Bar mitzvah* is 'son of the commandment.' Women used to not be allowed to read from the Torah. But now we can." Shayna smiles triumphantly.

Cherie claps her hands. "Very good! Women have worked hard to stand at the *bimah*. Like Miriam, women and girls have an important role in Judaism.

"Over the next months, you'll be preparing and learning, getting ready to open that door." She looks from Shayna to me. "When you open it, you'll discover that the path continues. There are rocky patches, deep valleys, and beautiful vistas. This longer path is your journey as a Jewish woman, as a part of the Jewish community. It is a lifelong journey, one that you're beginning now."

Shayna's eyes shine with excitement. My new friend is beginning her spiritual journey, a journey which will one day lead to her becoming an ordained *Rav Hazzan*, a rabbi cantor. There is certainty in her face; her Jewishness is a given. Certainty is something I don't have. I cannot contemplate my Jewishness without acknowledging that half of me is Catholic. I cannot contemplate my womanhood without acknowledging the two women who define me: my mother and my stepmother. When I imagine the steep path Cherie has laid out, I become overwhelmed by the idea of so many commandments, the *shoulds* and *musts* piling up on my shoulders.

This path was my mother's idea. When the topic came up a few months ago, I told her I didn't want a bat mitzvah. "Why not?" she asked. "It's an important ceremony, a rite of passage."

"Because I don't want all that attention," I said, a half-truth. "You should have seen Josh Schneider's bar mitzvah at that fancy country club, and the kids were jumping around, going wild. And then the DJ made everyone lift Josh up on a chair. I would hate that." I couldn't tell her that mostly I didn't want a bat mitzvah because I feel ashamed of my Jewishness, that I don't want to be a *tree*.

"We don't have to do something big," Mom said. "We can do it your way, something low-key. Only close friends and family." Half-heartedly, I agreed. Now, Mom is the one nudging me forward on this path, pulling me up, moving boulders out of my way. I reluctantly follow. Like the Star of David necklace she purchased and placed around my neck years earlier, the bat mitzvah will be her reminder to me of my daughterhood, my heritage. It will also be a reminder to my father and stepmother, who had once tried to take me away from her, who stand to erase my Jewishness.

See? she will say, looking pointedly at her ex-husband and his wife. *This is my daughter. And you can't have her.*

"So what does this *bat mitzvah* entail, anyways?" Krystal asks me. She enunciates the Hebrew words like they are a bite of something she wants to spit out. She's sitting at the kitchen table, doing her nails. In front of her is a box filled with little acrylic chips, organized by what finger they belong on. She takes one, dabs a little glue on it, and presses it onto a nailbed. Behind her, the window is open to let out the fumes. A fall chill enters the room.

"It's a Jewish ceremony for when you turn thirteen. There are some prayers and readings, a party at the end. It's just a few hours, no big deal," I say, trying to sound as casual as possible. "In fact, you guys don't even have to go if you don't want." I hope that my tone conceals what I actually mean, which is, *please don't go.*

"Of course, we're going. Unlike your other family, we actually do things together. Right, Matt?"

Dad turns from the couch where he and Sam are watching a Broncos game. "We'll be there. Can't miss an opportunity to see Ammi."

Krystal laughs, too gleefully to sound sincere. My stomach drops. When she laughs like this I try to shrink away, change the subject, hide. I know Dad dislikes my grandfather Ammi, whom I call Poppi. Back when he and Mom were married, Dad used to hate his ex-father-in-law's visits, accusing Ammi, who enjoyed a nomadic, carefree lifestyle, of habitually overstaying his welcome. Krystal dislikes Ammi for the undeniable facts of his existence: he is Mom's father, he is Jewish, and he is *weird*. Jewishness and weirdness are not tolerated in this family.

Ammi grew up in a conservative Jewish household, the son of a rabbi. And although he knows all the Jewish prayers and rituals, he is not religious in the strict sense of the word. He hangs Tibetan prayer flags and collects statues of the Buddha. People see his long, wiry hair and thick beard, his thrifted T-shirts, and they call him a "free spirit."

"Your mom told me we'll have parts to read in the ceremony. Krystie and I. Leo too," Dad says. Leo is Krystal's father. He is like a grandfather to me—a very traditional Italian Catholic grandfather.

I can feel my face growing hot, despite the cold breeze from the window. The toxic smell of glue is making me lightheaded.

"The ferret assigned us parts, did she?" Krystal says, filing down a freshly glued-on nail. "This will be fun."

Throughout the year ahead, I won't deliberately lie to my father and stepmother about the preparations for my bat mitzvah; I will just fail to mention almost everything. I will give them the bare minimum of details—enough so that they won't be taken by surprise by the invitation my mother will eventually send in the mail—an elegant glossy square of paper with pink watercolor irises and a matching RSVP card—but not too much so that they truly understand the significance of the event. I won't tell them about the weekly Hebrew lessons with my great aunt Hedy or the sessions with Cherie, and how she is sewing a *tallit* for me made from a soft purple fabric I picked out myself. And that on the *tallit* I have written in Hebrew a line from Jeremiah, "For I am with you." I don't mention my new friend Shayna, or our twin journeys to Jewish womanhood. I reassure myself that it doesn't matter to them. That they don't want to know. After all, they are uninterested in Jewish life.

At twelve years old, I am a master of obfuscation and omission, a tiny PR executive gliding on the line between truth and lie. I am so good that I don't even realize what I am doing. Sometimes I censor not just my words, but my own thoughts, so that later I will wonder if what I remember is an edited version of what actually occurred, safe for consumption.

On Mondays after school, Mom drops me off at my great aunt Hedy's house. We sit at her polished dining room table, the same table where we eat Rosh Hashanah dinners and break Yom Kippur fasts. On those days, the table is covered with a crisp white tablecloth, loaded with brisket, roasted potatoes, fresh honeycomb with apple slices, round challah studded with sweet raisins, or bagels, cream cheese, and lox, crudités arranged on platters, slices of halvah. Aunts and uncles and cousins crowd around the table, talking, laughing, praying. But during these Monday tutoring sessions, the house is hushed, save for the sound of our voices. On the table are pages of Hebrew, a silver tape recorder, and a crystal dish filled with dried strawberries which Hedy buys in bulk, knowing they're my favorite snack.

Hedy is Ammi's younger sister, and I marvel sometimes at the differences between them. For as long as I can remember, Aunt Hedy and her husband, my Uncle Michael, have lived in this immaculately clean house with dark wood, crisp white sofas, a bowl of fruit on gleaming granite countertops. I have never known my grandfather to stay in one place for long enough to own a sofa, or to bother with a fruit bowl. Sometimes he lives at a commune in New Mexico, sometimes he works as a park ranger in Hawaii. Often, he stays with friends who are spread out across the country, or with us. Ammi is theatrical, funny, extroverted. Hedy is soft-spoken, serious, religious. They often don't see eye to eye. There is a deeper history shared between them—of family secrets, infidelities, loyalty—that I don't understand yet. I think of Sam, three years younger than me, and how different we are, how we often bicker and provoke one another over stupid stuff. And yet I cannot imagine life without him. We are a unit, moving from Mom's to Dad's and back again in an endless cycle. Together. Maybe as we grow older, the differences will grow too. Maybe this is just how it is.

At the table, Hedy spreads out this week's reading while I chew on a dried strawberry. The silver tape recorder stands at the ready. Unlike Cherie, Hedy doesn't speak in metaphors. We might talk about school, or my friends, or Sam, but we don't talk about my path to Jewish womanhood. I know Mom has spoken to Hedy about my father and stepmother, how they take Sam and me to church with them, how we celebrate Easter and Christmas, how they once convinced me that I should live with them full time. Hedy must know that my path to Jewish womanhood is not linear, but full of pitfalls and traps. Mostly, we talk about the Hebrew—the dozens of prayers I will need to lead and recite, and the Torah and Haftarah portions I will chant at the *bimah*.

Though I learned the Hebrew alphabet in Saturday school at Temple Sinai and can read the words slowly by sounding them out, the Hebrew in the Torah and Haftarah is sung, not spoken. Little symbols above and below the letters, called *trope*, indicate different melodies. Hedy and I sing the melodies together—*merkha tipkha munakh*—then apply them to the readings. Whenever I stumble with pronunciation or sing the wrong trope, Hedy gently stops and corrects me. When finally I get the passage right, she makes me sing it three more times. Only then can I click "record" on the tape recorder, and sing the passage from beginning to end.

Back at Mom's house, the silver tape recorder lives on my desk in my bedroom. I replay it throughout the week, singing along with the recording of my own voice, then without it. Testing myself. Hedy wants me to be able to sight read the Hebrew and the tropes, but she also wants me to memorize my portions so that by the time I stand at the *bimah*, the words will be embedded within me, second nature. Each week I get better, and soon the Hebrew cantillations begin to flow like waves, one line cycling into the next. The words of *Pin'has* and

Yirmiyahu echo in my head. At Mom's house, I walk around chanting until Sam shouts at me to stop because he can't hear the TV. At Dad's, I find myself humming the melody under my breath. No one says anything—they probably think I'm humming a song from the radio. My father and stepmother don't know I can read Hebrew. I'm not sure if this is a secret or a lie by omission. I'm not sure I know the difference. I don't yet know that my self-censoring is a form of self-preservation.

Spring is here, and with it spring snowstorms. The flakes are large and wet. The snow piles up and melts within hours, leaving the suburban lawns in our neighborhood spongy and smelling fresh. The trees are budding, and bulbs are pushing through the soil. I am counting down the weeks until my thirteenth birthday on May 12, then my bat mitzvah on June 29.

The bat mitzvah planning has taken up all of Mom's free time. On weekends when Sam and I are at Dad's house, Mom goes to her office to cut and paste and copy the various sections of the program which she has painstakingly designed. *Birchot Hashahar*—Morning Blessings. *Shema U'virhoteha*—Call to Worship. *Amidah*—Entering God's Presence. She has assigned parts for each member of the family—even my second cousins. She has found a caterer and a venue for the service and reception. "I don't want a big bat mitzvah at the synagogue," I said, shuddering at the thought of my dad and stepmother sitting inside Temple Sinai, and so Mom found a small conference center in Evergreen, surrounded by a grassy meadow and views of the mountains. The air there is dry and smells like pine needles. She tracked down a cantor named Shaya, a friend of Poppi's, who lives in Boulder and has agreed to play the guitar and help lead the service. And she even found a low-budget DJ, someone who can play some Jewish music and light pop tunes for a brunch reception. Somehow Mom has even arranged for us to borrow a Torah that was damaged by the Nazis, but survived the Holocaust, now a refugee in Denver, Colorado.

The invitations have gone out and the RSVPs are rolling in. The momentum of the occasion is dizzying, like I am standing still and the world is hurtling forward without me.

I am sitting on Shayna's bed as she shows me the dress she's picked out for her bat mitzvah. It's black and made of a flowy material that hugs in at her waist. This is our first time hanging out outside of bat mitzvah preparations, and I am struck by the parallels in our worlds. Like me, Shayna lives in the suburbs, in a house with a similar layout to my dad's, but with Jewish art and iconography on the walls. Her younger sister is the same age as Sam.

"It's pretty," I say. "I really like it."

"Thanks," she says, swaying from side to side, swishing the skirt back and forth as she looks at her reflection in the mirror. We are both skinny, flat chested preteens, and yet once again, I am struck by the ease with which Shayna inhabits her body. While I hunch my shoulders protectively around my newly budding chest, Shayna holds her head high, her spine erect. Maybe, I think, it's the singing lessons.

"You really like black, don't you?" I say, smiling.

"What?"

"Your room—" I gesture to her walls, which are painted black. Pitch black. I had heard of brooding teenagers painting their rooms black out of spite, rebellion. I had thought this was a myth. But Shayna gets along just fine with her parents. She's not brooding at all. In fact, the more I've gotten to know her, the more I see how warm and even-keeled she is. Which is why the black walls surprise me.

She laughs. "Oh, right. I guess I do like black."

"Your parents let you paint your room black?" I don't even want to imagine what my stepmother would do if I covered my lilac bedroom walls in black paint. Mom might let me paint the walls black if I really begged. Then again, black walls aren't really my thing. Too dark, too somber.

"They don't mind. They bought the paint and let me paint it myself. I wanted it to feel cozy in here. Like a cave," she says. Somehow this response seems biblical to me.

"Have you gotten *your* dress yet?" Shayna asks.

"My mom and I got one from Dress Barn," I say, picturing the teal blue dress with the palm leaf pattern hanging in my closet. It's nice, the kind of modest, appropriate dress you'd find at a store associated with middle-aged lady work attire. I hadn't put much thought into it, because it's just a dress. Only as Shayna places her tallit over her shoulders and spins around to admire her reflection from all angles, do I realize how differently we are approaching our bat mitzvahs. Shayna can't wait to take her place at the *bimah*, to stand, shoulders back, arms open to a new chapter. Then there is me. I am gritting my teeth, hoping to make it through.

While Hedy teaches me to read and chant Hebrew, Poppi takes charge of my spiritual education. He has sent me letters all my life, in envelopes decorated with cut-out magazine photos. Now his letters contain historical lessons, quotes to meditate upon, instructions for how to write my *Dvar Torah*, my bat mitzvah speech. He sends me a Hebrew alphabet book. *Dear Lauren, A letter a day. Meditate on the letters. They are thousands of years old and have accumulated great meaning. And they are beautiful. Love, Poppi*

Sometimes I return from Dad's house to a small stack of envelopes waiting for me on my bed. I don't rush to open them, knowing they will contain more lessons and ideas to integrate into my already overflowing brain.

When Poppi visits, we sit at Mom's kitchen table and he teaches me about the history of the Jewish people. He draws a timeline and marks dates on it: *1280 B.C.E. Jewish exodus from Egypt. 965–928 B.C.E. Reign of Solomon. 950 B.C.E First temple built.* These dates are abstractions for me, and I slog through these lessons about the history of

Israel and its various kings, the repeated destruction and rebuilding of the temple. During these sessions in the kitchen, Poppi's usual silly self disappears. He becomes stern, didactic, and I think I can catch glimpses of his and Hedy's upbringing, of the ancestral lessons which must have permeated their childhood, of their strict mother and overworked rabbi father, their scholarly grandfather who lived with the family and spent hours each day studying the Talmud and writing in biblical Hebrew, of their kosher kitchen, and their phone ringing off the hook with the calls of needy congregants.

But then Poppi gives me a copy of Anne Frank's diary, tells me to read it. And I do. I devour *The Diary of a Young Girl* in one weekend, holed up in my bedroom at Mom's. I am struck by Anne's honesty and her life inside the secret annex with her family. I see myself in her, even though our lives are impossibly different. Her annex is both prison and life raft. Inside it, Anne is isolated from the world, and yet she discovers that the annex contains a whole world of its own.

While reading, I often pause and close the book in order to stare at the girl's photo on the cover—her dark eyes, shoulder-length hair, wry smile. I try to imagine her face, her voice, her hands, her laugh. She could be my friend. She could be Shayna. The final words of the book are full of grief, but also recognition. I know she and her family are taken to concentration camps, and that she will die there, that only her father and her diary will survive. I know this, and yet I see myself, a nearly thirteen-year-old girl reflected back in her words:

> I get cross, then sad, and finally end up turning my heart inside out, the bad part on the outside and the good part on the inside, and I keep trying to find a way to become what I'd like to be and what I could be if . . . if only there were no other people in the world.

One afternoon, Cherie has Shayna and me press our hands onto paper, outline them in pencil, then decorate the page with designs that reflect how we feel in that moment. They are *hamsas*, supposed to protect and bring good fortune. I draw a pair of serene and watchful eyes, a cloud of purple, a book, a geometric design. In barely legible silver gel pen, I write a stream-of-consciousness string of words that wraps around the outline of my hand. The words flow, a river of worry and contradiction and ambivalence. I am surprised to read the last sentences, as though my hand wrote them of its own accord: *Sometimes I think I'm too selfish and sometimes I think I'm too sympathetic. But mostly I am too selfish.*

Too full of feeling, too selfish. I would make myself transparent if I could, or better yet, a green screen onto which others—my father and stepmother, Poppi, Mom, Hedy, Cherie—could project their desires and needs. I could become what they want me to become, think the way they want me to think. But every time I try to be less selfish, to be less of *myself*, I fail. My heart flips bad side out. Someone, or everyone, is unhappy.

At Dad's house, my bat mitzvah preparations fade into the background of family dinners, spring sports, and trips to see my stepmother's family. For Easter, we drive two hours south to Cañon City to visit Leo, whom Sam and I call "Grandpa." Visits with Leo are always the same. We watch Rockies games on the patio TV, take walks along the river, and visit with his buddies, old guys who tell knee-slapping stories then give Sam and me each a crisp five-dollar bill.

We've been coming to my step-grandparents' house since I was just six years old. The teal green carpet, the pink-tiled bathroom, and the smell of the garage refrigerator where Leo's baitworms live in Styrofoam containers is as familiar to me as Aunt Hedy's polished table. Just six months earlier, Leo's wife Phyllis died unexpectedly. The house is emptier now, but Leo is still full of warmth, always ready with a joke and a sly smile.

On Easter, we make his family's traditional Italian ravioli. He dusts his dining room table with a thick layer of flour, then unwraps a big log of chilled pasta dough. Sam and I take turns cranking the handle of the pasta machine, while Leo cradles the flattened dough in his calloused palms, putting it through again and again, as each time the dough gets a little longer and thinner.

"Back in the day, we didn't have pasta machines, just a big table and a broomstick. My mother did all this by hand," Leo says, gently laying the long sheet of pasta on the table. His round belly is sprinkled white with flour. "We also had to walk to school in the snow with hot potatoes in our pockets, and it was uphill both ways." He winks at me and I laugh, though I've heard this line many times before. Behind him on the wall hangs a carved wooden crucifix and a porcelain plate on which the Ten Commandments are printed in gold script.

Once the pasta dough is flattened into sheets, we measure out spoonfuls of filling—a mixture of ground beef, spinach, and mozzarella cheese—and paint the edges of the dough with water. Then we fold the pasta onto itself, cut, and seal each ravioli with the tines of a fork. Tonight, Leo will make a pot of tomato sauce and simmer a round of beef braciola. Tomorrow, we'll eat our Italian meal for supper after Easter mass.

Since that first meeting with Cherie, I have felt a low level of inner turmoil about going to mass, knowing that I am now actively on the path to Jewish womanhood. I have not told Shayna that I am also Catholic, and I wonder what she would think of me, going to church and making Easter ravioli when I'm supposed to be studying the Torah. Now I wonder what Leo would think of me if he knew I was chanting Hebrew, learning the Jewish prayers. If I were to tell him, would he still let me come to mass, would he still tell me stories about his devout Italian mother? What will Krystal and Dad say, when they see the *tree* I am growing into?

These are the thoughts that swirl through me like a sandstorm as I dip my fingers in the holy water at Leo's church, St. Michael's, cross myself (forehead, sternum, left shoulder, right shoulder), settle into a long wooden pew, kneel (hands folded, eyes on the crucifix), and pray to Jesus, or God, or one of the two. *Lord help me*, I always start. *Help me to be a better daughter. Help me to tell the truth. Help me find who I am. Help me find you.*

I know the words of the Lord's prayer, when to cross myself and when to kneel, when to say *Peace be with you*. Compared to Judaism, Catholicism is straightforward—no second language to learn, no chant to decipher, no hidden meanings to unearth and endlessly discuss, only a handful of holidays to celebrate. There is only the concept of the Holy Trinity, which still confuses me. Is Jesus God or son or both? And what, or who, is the Holy Spirit?

I yearn for Anne Frank's simple and beautiful conception of God: "The best remedy for those who are afraid, lonely or unhappy is to go outside, somewhere where they can be quite alone with the heavens, nature and God." And yet, while she was in the annex, she couldn't go outside at all, couldn't feel this simple remedy for her fear and loneliness. Perhaps we always imagine God to be in the places we are not.

I was seven, Sam was four, when my father and stepmother first started taking us to mass. They had just moved back to Colorado, after living in Houston for a few years. Mom was furious.

"You are Jewish," she would tell me. "Your father agreed to raise you Jewish. It is inappropriate for you to go to church."

"Your mom wants us to change who we are," Krystal would say. "She wants us to leave you out, to exclude you. But you like going to mass, don't you?"

At first, I agreed with Mom. *It's inappropriate*, I said, repeating her word. But I soon learned that Sam and I would be made to feel different, not a part of the family, unless we went to mass, too. Our Jewishness was something that held my father and stepmother back from being who *they* wanted to be. If Sam and I couldn't go to mass, then our father and stepmother would be forced to skip mass too, forced to commit a mortal sin. But it wasn't our fault. It was Judaism's fault, my mother's fault for making us this way and making their lives so difficult. I learned to leave my Jewishness at the front door to their house, like taking off a pair of dirty boots. I didn't want to be different.

In the beginning, I was afraid that the parishioners at the church would know Sam and I were Jewish, as if at birth we were marked by a yellow star for everyone to see. When we stumbled over the words of the Lord's Prayer, when we clumsily tried to copy the sign of the cross, I kept waiting for someone to point and say "Impostors! They're not allowed to be here!" I imagined the priest would then stop the mass, and Sam and I would have to leave, our heads hanging low. But no one said a thing. And I realized that no one could tell. No one knew my secret. And this became its own shameful power, the power to shapeshift. To be Jewish and Catholic. To move between my parents' worlds, a vessel of secrets.

The sky is bright blue and cloudless, like blown glass, ready to shatter. I shower, put on the teal blue dress, brush my hair, apply lip gloss. Chant the words to *Yirmiyahu*, chant the words to *Pin'has*. I haven't needed the silver tape recorder in over a month. At our last Monday session, Hedy told me I was ready. She has lent me her *yad*, like a pen, except at the end, there is a tiny silver hand pointing with its index finger. I will use it, instead of my own finger, to keep my place when I read from the Torah scrolls. The text is sacred; you can't touch the parchment.

Mom comes out of her bedroom, her face glowing. She is freshly showered too, her dark, wet hair hanging in thick ropes. She's wearing a new mauve dress and silver earrings.

"Today's the day," she says, sing-song. "You look beautiful, sweetie. Are you ready?" she kisses the top of my head.

"I think so," I say. "I'm nervous."

"Don't be nervous. You'll do great. You've prepared all year." She goes into Sam's bedroom. I hear her speaking to him softly, telling him it's time to get up. She's laid out his outfit on a chair—khaki pants, white collared shirt, clip-on tie, blue *kippah*.

Yesterday, the family arrived, and we gathered in our house. My aunts and uncles. Grandma Joan. Poppi. Aunt Hedy and Uncle Michael. Their children. Even my second cousins who live in Connecticut and Maryland. My second cousin Samantha, who had her bat mitzvah last year, told me that it was the best night of her life. Her parents had rented out a hotel ballroom for the reception, and there were hundreds of people there.

"Just wait until the end, when you get to open all the gifts," she told me conspiratorially.

Together, we celebrated Shabbat. We lit the candles, said the *Kiddush* and the *Hamotzi*. Mom had ordered catering, and we ate challah, chicken piccata and roasted potatoes and salad, and Sam and the boy cousins drank too much soda and darted around the tables, chocolate chip cookies in hand. My mother was animated and alive; her laughter, loud and piercing, rose above the din. All her planning and organizing had paid off. Even Cecil seemed to be having a good time, engrossed in conversation with Mom's cousin Ben. I allowed myself to get caught up in the celebration, to talk and giggle with Samantha. My family was here. I felt ready.

Now, on the morning of the big day, the house is buzzing with motion. Mom is the air traffic controller, directing us to carry coolers full of ice, programs, various bags of supplies. My grandma Joan, who is staying at our house, seems worried. Her mouth is a thin, taut line. She keeps asking my mother questions, calling my mother's name, the last syllable stretched out like a banner: "Saraaaa, do you need this? Saraaaa, shall I grab this? Saraaaa, do you have tissues?" I wonder if it's because she has to see Poppi—her ex-husband—and his family. All the old hurts and jealousies rising to the surface. I've watched as Mom does her best to keep her parents on opposite sides of the room, paying special attention to my grandmother so she doesn't feel left out. I know what Mom is doing, because it's what I do, too. Divorce—even one that happened decades earlier—is a scar that never completely heals.

Last night, as I was getting ready for bed, I overheard Grandma Joan and Mom in the kitchen.

"Sara, are *they* coming?" my grandmother asked in a low voice. My ears perked up. I knew exactly who *they* referred to.

"Yes, they'll be there. I couldn't *not* invite them, Mom." Her words were terse, staccato. My grandmother was silent for a moment.

"Well, I hope they don't make a scene," she said finally.

"They better not."

Maybe everything will be okay, I think, as I grip the edges of the music stand that serves as my makeshift *bimah*. A roomful of family and friends look back at me, their faces brightened by the mountain sunshine that pours through floor-to-ceiling windows. Today the Evergreen conference center, with its institutional gray carpet and padded folding chairs, has turned into a *shul*. Our ark is a folding table covered in white linen. The Torah rests there, dressed in regal blue velvet. This morning, Hedy showed me the exact place where I will read from its parchment scroll.

Shaya has finished tuning his guitar. Sam and our cousin Eric have passed out programs to all the guests. My heart beats fast; my stomach tightens.

Mom approaches the *bimah*, gives me a little smile. She's wearing her dark lipstick; her cheeks are colored with blush. She adjusts the microphone and reads a welcome speech from the inside of her program.

"Becoming a Bat Mitzvah is a milestone event in a young person's life and requires enormous preparation. Today marks the day that this remarkable young woman will take her place in the Jewish community as a *full* member. We are here to celebrate the goodness of life and the passage that Lauren is making into her womanhood. We are so proud of her!"

I glance at Dad and Krystal, who at this moment are surely beginning to realize how much I have not told them about my bat mitzvah. Dad is dressed in a nice work suit, his hands folded in his lap. Krystal wears a black linen dress. Her eyes are glued to my mother's face—her thin, red lips frozen in a tight smile. Leo looks bewildered. I doubt that he has ever been around this many Jewish people in his life. There's no synagogue in Cañon City, and maybe no Jews there at all.

Later, after my stepmother bans me from going to mass and my father accuses me of lying to their faces, I will comb back through my memories of this day. I will dissect every facial movement, every word spoken. Looking through the photos, I will notice that almost all the guests were dressed in colorful summer clothing. Even the men donned brightly embroidered *kippahs* and prayer shawls. Only my father and stepmother were dressed in all black as if attending a wake. But the beauty of the present moment is that there is no knowledge of what is to come. The future is still unwritten. And today, my Catholic father, stepmother, and step-grandfather are but a small island in a sea of *kippah*-covered heads, the few *goys* amidst the Kohns and Weinbergs and Schwartzes and Bergers. They are outnumbered by *trees*. Today, Krystal's normally outsized presence is diminished by the forest.

Mom picks up the soft purple *tallit* that Cherie has made for me and holds it out in her arms.

"Among our most elemental human need is the need for shelter," she says. "Before life itself, we begin in the shelter of our mother's womb, and throughout our life we associate shelter with this most basic kind of protection. It is thus natural that we Jews, like in many other religious traditions, don a prayer shawl during the act of worship. It helps us feel God's enveloping presence."

I wrap the *tallit* around my shoulders. Traditionally, only men wear a prayer shawl, but Cherie told Shayna and me that gender shouldn't limit the expression of our faith and traditions. I am grateful for the weight of the fabric on my body, like a warm, settling embrace. The hand-tied *tzit tzit* nearly touch the floor.

"*Baruch atah Adonai, eloheynu melech ha'olam asher kideshanu behmitzvotavav vetzivanu lehitatef batzitzit,*" I say. *Blessed is the source of shelter, enveloping and protecting us, helping us to feel God's loving presence when we pray.*

The ceremony continues smoothly. My anxiety has dissipated and I read confidently—not too fast, not too slow, the way I practiced with Hedy at her dining room table. I push the doubts and fears about Dad and Krystal to the back of my mind, storing them there for later. *Everything is okay. Everything is going to be okay. I am here.* I chant from the miracle Torah that outlasted the Nazis. The ancient letters dance beneath Hedy's silver *yad*.

I think there is a small chance that today my father and stepmother will see me in my fullest expression. Church girl *and* bat mitzvah girl. Maybe my performance will win them over. Maybe they will see that religion is something I *do*, not something I am. But even I don't know that yet.

My *Dvar Torah*, my sermon, or speech, is about responsibility. While writing it, I decided there were three kinds of responsibility: responsibility to your community, to your family, and to your individual self. This last piece was the most difficult for me to parse. How could I be responsible to my *self*? I hold the seven typed pages before me, with my last-minute edits in pencil. When I practiced this in the mirror, the words sounded authoritative, convincing. *Be like Jeremiah, be like Elijah. Know who you are. Listen to the voice within you.* Now, as I say them aloud, I realize I have no idea how to do this, that I have never heard God's voice. The words ring hollow.

> Individual responsibility is knowing who you are and what you want. Jeremiah knew who he was as soon as G-D talked to him. He didn't

try to deny it; he was born to be a messenger of G-D. The prophet Elijah's message was not so clear, and yet still he listened. Ahab and Jezebel were looking for him in order to kill him. Elijah ran into the wilderness to find G-D. All around him are earthquakes, fire, and wind, but even then he was able to hear the still, small voice inside of him that was G-D. In Hebrew this is *Kol D'Mamah Sh'ketah*. Honesty with yourself and the still small voice inside of you are the same thing because they are both part of G-D.

As quickly as the ceremony begins, it is over. Endorphins and relief rush over me like cool water. My relatives hug me. Poppi places a rough hand on top of my head. "Well done, kid, well done," he says. Hedy wipes tears out of the corners of her eyes. She tells me she is proud of me, and that she'll miss our Monday afternoons together. My middle school friends gather in the adjacent room where a buffet of brunch food—blintzes, eggs, roasted potatoes, fresh fruit—is ready to eat. We sit at tables on the deck outside and drink in the mountain air. Mom comes around with a camera. She is radiant, victorious. "There's my gorgeous girl," she says. "You did so good. I'm so proud of you." I look up at her and smile. *Click. Click.* Sam and Eric zoom by. They could be brothers, fraternal twins even: two Jewish boys with shiny, chestnut-colored hair, dark eyes, *yarmulkes* askance.

I haven't seen Mom this happy in a long time. Together, we have reached the door at the top of the steep pathway. I have officially stepped through the doorway to womanhood, taken my place in the Jewish community beside her. But I feel the same. I still feel like a child, stuck in my same familiar skin. Cherie said that my lifelong journey would begin now. But from here, my path splits in two; each direction leads into the woods, dense and dark. If only I could pause for a moment and listen to the still, small voice inside me. I know I could hear the voice clearly, if only there were no other people in the world.

Parenting Diary: Barnes & Noble

November 8, 2000—Sam had his soccer party in the evening, but I decided to take Lauren out to dinner and the bookstore to buy books and talk to her. In the car, I explained again to her that she is not the one to make the rules and decide where she is going to be. I told her the parenting time schedule is a court order, and we all have to obey it. Lauren asked "Mom, why can't kids decide on the schedule?" I again told her that she is a child, and this schedule is determined by her dad and me.

I told her we were all going to see a psychologist who would help us figure out what was the best arrangement. I asked her why she was doing this, taking the bus to her dad's house when she was supposed to come to my house. She said, "I miss my dad," which is what she always says. Then she said that what she really wanted was to live with her dad and see me every other weekend. She said this would only be fair because she had been seeing me more for most of her life, and she felt it should be switched now. She said that if she didn't like it, then we could just go back to the way it is now. I didn't say anything at that point because I was so taken aback. The original agenda with Matt had been 50 percent (of which he currently has 46 percent). I told her I would think about it, and we would talk about it with the psychologist, but for now we had to stick to the current schedule. I tried to control my emotions, and we went to the bookstore and out to dinner without discussing this anymore. Lauren was very friendly at the restaurant and talked about school and her friends.

When we got home, Lauren received a phone call from Krystal almost *immediately. I could tell she was quizzing Lauren about what was going on and Lauren was trying to reply surreptitiously. When Lauren told her we had gone to dinner at The Sahara, a Lebanese restaurant that is one of my favorites, I heard Lauren saying several times, "No it was really good, honest. No, Middle Eastern food is really good, Krystie."*

I want everyone to get their fair share. I want bad people to be punished and good people to be rewarded. I want the pie to be divvied up carefully, equally—everyone leaves with a slice, everyone leaves happy. In school I learn to *share*. At home, I learn that I am a thing to be shared, that I have to share my *self*. But since I cannot parcel my body into pieces, I divvy up the next best thing: my time and my love. It's only fair.

My stepmother tells me: *Your birth mom thinks you don't have room in your heart to love more people, but guess what—you have room in your heart to love as many people as you want. There is not a finite amount of love.* I believe my stepmother, though she often twists my mother's words around and around until I wonder if my mother is a bad person, unworthy of love. When my stepmother says *I love you, Pumpkin*, I tell her that I love her back. I believe her when she says my heart has room for everyone, that there is no need to measure it out, cut it into pieces. I imagine my heart like a hot air balloon, expanding and rising, carrying my whole family inside its basket. But when I look for evidence of that infinite love, I find not a rising balloon, but a labyrinth of partitions and corridors that lead to dark, empty rooms.

In the bookstore, though, among the smell of paper and ink and the cozy green carpet, the partitions lower, the corridors widen until there are no walls at all, only stories. I run my fingers over the glossy spines of books—each containing a universe to explore. Fairness is a concept that does not exist in this place where ideas multiply like cells, where the resources are infinite. A *Wrinkle in Time, Jacob Have I Loved, Hatchet, Bridge to Terabithia, Stargirl, Number the Stars, Holes.*

I pluck the books from the shelves, their covers bright like ripe fruits. I watch as the cashier scans each barcode, gently places each book into the plastic shopping bag. Mom opens her wallet—overflowing with receipts and cards—writes a check and cleanly tears it off. She looks over at me with a sad smile.

    The problem with fairness is that you can divide and divide and divide until there is nothing left of you but crumbs. Only when you retreat into the world of imagination do you become whole again.

Little Brother, Little Sister

Once upon a time, a baby boy was born in Denver, Colorado. He was dense as a torpedo, with walnut brown eyes and limbs like fat sausages ready to burst from their casings. The baby wailed, red-faced and kicking, wisps of dark hair matted across his forehead. He had been born ten days early—induced—because he was so big and was causing his mother all sorts of problems. Perhaps he was upset at being forced into this new and unfamiliar world. Perhaps he felt exposed. His sister, three years and three days older, was unsympathetic and tired of the crying. She asked her mother if they could take him back to the hospital. "No," her mother said, and so the sister returned to the couch where she proceeded to watch Sesame Street *with her fingers in her ears.*

This is the story I knew from my brother's birth, the story I was told—Sam's angry cries, and my disappointment that the crier was here to stay. From the time he was born, Sam was hungry; nursing was one of the few things that calmed him. He ate so voraciously that at the end of a feeding, he would be gasping for air, like a diver surfacing to breathe. He grew quickly, and soon he was waddling around on stout legs, climbing onto furniture, then falling and crying, then getting back up again. Once, Mom went to wake him from a nap, and found him standing upright on top of his dresser, ready to jump into the air.

My brother was not the quiet playmate I had imagined he would be. I explored my world through words and pictures and careful observation. I liked to read books—or be read to—and create convoluted storylines for my dolls. I liked to do puzzles and draw intricate pictures of princesses in long, colorful dresses. Sam could be convinced to do these things, too, but only for short periods of time. Mostly, he needed to test the physical boundaries of the world, to press his body up against them. He wanted a tactile blueprint of his surroundings. And his strong emotions bubbled just below the surface, ready to erupt at any moment. From the day he was born, our roles as siblings seemed predetermined, archetypal. We were Yin and Yang. We loved each other fiercely, and we were often at war.

As Sam grew into a toddler, my parents' marriage disintegrated. Already, the woman who would become my stepmother had been hovering at the periphery of our family. I had met Krystal shortly after Sam was born, when I accompanied my father to his downtown office with a box of blue bubblegum cigars. "It's a boy," I said, reciting my lines to each of my father's coworkers as we made the rounds. "I have a little brother." I repeated the words to a woman in the accounting department who wore a fitted pencil skirt, a matching blazer with gold buttons, and stiletto heels. Her teased hair rested on her padded shoulders like a blonde cloud. Her nails were long and red, and very shiny. *Barbie* is what her coworkers called her—for all the obvious reasons—but my father called her *Kar*, her initials.

I don't remember that meeting with Krystal (after all, I was barely three years old), but years later she would recount her memory of the moment often enough that it would become inscribed in my imagination, like I was watching a movie reel of my own life. I see myself: small, with a button nose and a chopped bob. My blue eyes match my father's, who, on this day, is dressed casually in jeans and a collared shirt. His face radiates with pride, the pride of fatherhood, but also something else I can't quite place. Some energy passes between him and the woman with the long, red nails. I don't know her, yet she is both familiar and menacing; her lipsticked smile covers the lower half of her face like a mask. In my sticky, outstretched hand, the stale blue bubblegum cigar is a symbolic offering, a sacrifice. *It's a boy.*

Italo Calvino might call the bubble gum in my hand a "magical object." "I would say that the moment an object appears in a narrative," he writes in *Six Memos for the Next Millennium*, "it is charged with a special force and becomes like the pole of a magnetic field, a knot in the network of invisible relationships." Of course, Calvino was writing about fiction and fable, but why couldn't the narrative of a life—of a family—be similarly charged with magic and symbolism? The bubblegum cigar changes hands, and the world tilts.

Years later, Krystal would wistfully recall this day, saying: "All I could think was 'darn, this man just had another baby. He must really love his wife.'" Then she would give my father a sly look, one that said, *But he loved me more.*

The stories that our parents tell about us from the time before we remember have the quality of a dream. After Sam was born, my father took me on a camping trip in the mountains. He tells me that on this trip I tugged on his sleeve and told him that I'd found a patch of wild strawberries. "Wild strawberries?" he repeated, doubting my claim. "Come on, I'll show you," I said. He followed me, looked down to where I pointed, and sure enough, there they were, the ruby red fruits fragrant and barely larger than my thumbnail. The next day, we went fishing at Chicago Lakes. A photo of us shows Dad kneeling in jeans and a sweatshirt, his white socks peeking through Birkenstock sandals. I am chubby cheeked, standing very upright. Together, we hold up a string of about six rainbow trout; the trout on my side nearly touch the dusty ground. I remember the way the fishing line had danced in the water, and the sudden understanding that there existed an entire world beneath the surface, hidden from view. In this dark, wet world the fish lived and swam and hunted for food before being yanked, gasping, into the light.

My father and I had rainbow trout and wild strawberries, three years' worth of shared experiences and stories. We had a bond. In psychology, this relationship would be called "attachment," a term coined by psychologist John Bowlby to describe the primary bond created between a child and one or, at most, a few adults. In *The Body Keeps the Score*, Bessel van der Kolk writes that "[t]he more responsive the adult is to the child, the deeper the attachment." This bond between parent and child, he says, is "the secure base from which a child moves out into the world." I had an adoring and attentive mother and father; my base was secure.

But by the time Sam arrived, our family circumstances had shifted. The marriage was failing. My father was finishing his MBA, attending night classes and working late. After the divorce, my mother, writing to her lawyer and a family psychologist, claimed that my father never formed an attachment with Sam. According to my mother, he had seemed uninterested in Sam then, annoyed at his incessant crying. Could it have been that Dad's dissatisfaction with his marriage was negatively affecting his ability to bond with his new son? I know he loved Sam, but perhaps he was also distracted by new ambitions, new prospects. Shortly after Sam's first birthday, Dad announced he was unhappy and moved out.

One of the few stories my father tells about my brother from before the divorce involves a potted plant. According to Dad, Sam became fascinated with a large ficus tree that lived by a sunny window in the dining room. If no one was looking, Sam would methodically grab fistfuls of the pot's soil and dump it on the wood floor, like a tiny scientist studying the phenomenon of cause and effect. When our father discovered what Sam had done, he lightly slapped Sam's chubby little hand with his own. "Ta ta," he said, one slap per syllable. Sam then cried, either out of repentance or outrage. Dad swept up the soil and put it back in the pot. But soon, Sam was back at the plant—a pile of dirt on the ground, his hands literally soiled with evidence. "Ta ta," our father would say again and again, each slap a little harder than the one before, and each time the cycle would begin again.

Dad was teaching Sam the concept of consequences and self-regulation. Or, in psychological terms, he was teaching his son to "tolerate higher levels of arousal." Van der Kolk notes that fathers often take on this regulatory parental role. "The tough love program," Dad called it as we got older, though Sam's program seemed tougher than mine. Dad had all sorts of these sayings, maxims from pop culture and politics which he translated into parenting edicts. He was the "800-pound gorilla." He believed you needed to "trust but verify." And pick your friends wisely, because "if you fly with the crows, you get shot with the crows." *Ta ta.*

The potted plant story revealed another telling difference between Sam and me. One *ta ta*, and I would never have touched the soil again. But Sam could not or would not resist his impulses; he would risk punishment to follow his curiosity. Later, when we were teenagers, I would admire and fear this trait of his. His needs—for affection, freedom, sustenance—seemed unruly, even dangerous. I, on the other hand, was skilled at self-deprivation. To survive, I would curl inside my shell, tamp down my own impulses, writing about them in my notebook. *Look*, I wanted to say to Sam, *see how I do it? How I bide my time avoiding trouble?* But my brother had no shell. He wore his fears and desires like a second skin. Had Sam been Hansel and I Gretel, he would have happily gorged himself on the witch's candy house; I would have starved rather than eat a single sugary shingle, for fear that I would be jailed for property damage.

Despite our distinct desires and personalities, we existed as a singular entity: infuriatingly familiar, intrinsically different. Each held a mirror up to the other's existence. We intuited each other's thoughts and feelings and insecurities. We loved and hated each other in the same minute, in the same moment. Even now, a thousand miles apart, we move through the world independently, and yet we remain connected by an invisible, inextricable, unbreakable thread.

As a child, Sam was my constant in a world of shifting variables. Together, we bounced between Mom's house and Dad's house. We were not the deprived, orphaned children of fairy tales—everyone seemed to want us *too* much. And there was nothing magical about the suburb we moved to shortly before I started second grade. The closest thing we had to a fairy tale forest was Cherry Creek State Park, where red-tailed hawks circled over vast prairie dog fields, and ragged clumps of cottonwood trees grew by the murky man-made lake. Our world was safe and sprawling and open to the sky. Still, when I picture Sam and me as children, I see two siblings hand in hand, tromping through an enchanted forest—ominous and wild—together.

I may have been a loyal sister, but I was not a good sister. Like a fairy tale villain, I could be cruel, vindictive, cunning. At Mom's house, I would needle Sam endlessly, knowing my words would provoke him to lash out with his fists. When he inevitably did, I would cry, whether or not I was actually in pain. Mom or Cecil would reprimand Sam for using physical force—"don't hit, use your words"—but they were frustratingly soft when it came to consequences. A thirty-minute time-out in your bedroom with all your toys was not satisfactory to me. "Punish him!" I would demand. "Punish him or he'll become a wife beater!" Where had I learned the term "wife beater?" And why was I so bloodthirsty? All I knew was that a wife beater seemed like the worst possible thing for a boy to become. I wanted to see Sam suffer for what he had done. I wanted him to be locked up. I wanted *consequences*.

In one of my early memories of my brother and me, we are in a cabin room with Lincoln log walls and two queen-sized beds. One bed is for my mother and Cecil, and one bed is for Sam and me. The cabin is in a national park in the mountains. We have driven here from Denver in Mom's green Subaru hatchback, and now we are surrounded by a forest of pines and shivering aspens. It is summer, and outside the sun warms the cabin walls, which are sticky in places with sap. For some reason, Mom and Cecil have left Sam and me alone in the room. Perhaps Mom is in the bathroom and Cecil is bringing in supplies from the car, or maybe they are getting maps and water from the front desk. Whatever the reason, we are temporarily by ourselves, and Sam is making me mad.

"Children who are bad get punished," I tell him. "And you're being bad." I can't be more than five years old, but I'm bigger and stronger. There are no adults here, and so I do what I believe an adult would do to a bad child. I make my brother lie face down on the bed, then I pull down his elastic-waisted pants, and whack his bare butt with my hand. *Thwack, thwack, thwack!*

Immediately my anger subsides, and a strange, sinking sensation takes its place. I do not yet know the words for guilt, remorse, shame. What I do know is that Sam is a little boy. And I am a big, mean girl. The awareness washes over me uncomfortably. He is crying, and I pull up his pants and hug him to me. I want to take back what I've done, erase it, but I can't. Instead, I hug him, hoping he'll forgive me. "It's okay, it's okay," I whisper. "I'm sorry. It's okay."

In his book on fairy tales, *The Uses of Enchantment*, Bettelheim notes that "when we are young, whatever we feel at the moment fills our entire existence. Becoming aware that he feels two ways about something at the same time—for example, when the child wants to grab the cookie, but also wants to obey Mother's order not to—confuses the child." I loved my brother, and I wanted to hurt him. But hurting him only led me to feel shame and regret. These strong, intertwined emotions were confusing. No relationship up until this point had revealed more about my warring impulses—what Bettelheim calls the child's "dual nature." No other person in my life could turn a single moment into an entire existence.

I realize now that I commanded my mother to punish Sam because

I knew she wouldn't do it. "He's in time-out in his room, that's fine for now," she would say—patient, exasperated—while I, the tyrant, fumed. She was teaching me an important lesson: it's okay to have strong emotions, but it's not always okay to act on those emotions. People do things in anger that they later regret. Hadn't I learned this already? In this house, Mom was the safeguard for my bloodlust, the buffer for my anger.

At Dad's house, however, there was no buffer, and punishment for bad behavior—real or imagined—was severe and drawn out, a complex ritual. As Sam and I got older, there were no simple groundings or time-outs, but rather an inscrutable system of major and minor infractions and their corresponding lectures and yelling, or silent treatments, temporary exclusion, withholding of food.

Almost worse than the punishment itself was the build-up to it.

The first clue that you had done something wrong was when you walked in the front door, and Krystal turned her head away at the obligatory hello kiss, offering you a dry cheek instead of her thin, pursed lips. Then the heavy, awkward silence as she cooked dinner and you set the table, a silence punctuated only by the sounds of clinking silverware and sizzling garlic, in which you made a mental list of every possible bad thing you might have done in the last forty-eight hours. You may have signed up for marching band instead of cross country without consulting her first, or forgotten to take out the trash and recycling, or ridden your bike through mud and failed to clean the tires before parking it in the garage. The opportunities to fuck up increased exponentially as you got older. Eventually, you'd start on your homework at your desk upstairs, a dull ache in your gut. *You've been bad.*

After a while you'd feel the low rumble of the garage door beneath the floor of your bedroom. Dad's home. Exhaust fumes and a rush of cold air would enter the house; you'd greet him sheepishly while searching his face for clues. Krystal would call out to him in a sing-song voice, then plant an overly romantic kiss on his lips, as if to say "everything is great with us, it's *you* that's the problem." Then she would pour two cosmopolitan martinis with lite cranberry juice—one for her, one for him. And you would all sit down for dinner—lasagna and salad, or beef stroganoff, or chicken parmesan. You'd force down a glass of whole milk while they drank red wine. The sounds of Norah Jones or Frank Sinatra would float up from the CD player in the living room, barely audible over the sound of your own heart beating in your throat.

Then they would give each other a look, and the prelude would make way to the preamble, the tense atmosphere would electrify, and Krystal would meet your eyes for the first time all day with a stare so hard and cold, all you could do was brace yourself, twisting your napkin while your knuckles turned white. Anything could happen next. The list of possibilities expanded as time went on, as Krystal became more volatile, more dissatisfied—with you, with this family, with her life. You might be lectured and belittled, then sent to your room where you'd cry until you fell asleep, waking with swollen eyes. Or you might be backed up against a wall, one of your stepmother's long fingernails shoved into your sternum, her sour wine breath filling your nostrils. And worse—far worse—you might not even be the one getting punished tonight.

In my worst memory, I watch from behind a corner—paralyzed—as my brother's face is slapped again and again and *again*. I hear the dull thud of a hand against Sam's cheek, his choking sobs, the pee trickling down his child's legs. I want to run out from my hiding place, to wedge my body in front of my brother's, but I am immobile, sinking in quicksand.

No, deep down, I knew that neither of us deserved any of that. And so at Dad's, Sam and I still bickered, but out of sight of the adults. We fought, but never tattled. My wrath only simmered, undone by a low-level and ever-present fear. I found a place inside myself where I could lock my anger and resentment away. Though we were only blocks from her house, Mom was inaccessible here, as distant as a dream. Here, Sam and I were like the motherless children of fairy tales. Neither of us wanted to be responsible for getting the other in trouble, so we remained a team. *The children.* We had to.

I have always been drawn to fairy tales. As a child, my aunt Hedy gave me a thick volume of Hans Christian Andersen stories. Sam and I begged Mom to read the most awful ones again and again. We loved the one about the little girl with red shoes whose feet can't stop dancing, and who begs a kindly executioner to chop them off. We listened in awe to the story of another little girl who warms herself with matches, lighting one at a time, until the matches run out and she freezes to death in the snow. We didn't pick up on the tales' warped paternalism; we simply delighted in their gruesomeness. Mom complained that the fairy tales were giving her nightmares, and we believed her. She often had nightmares in those days, ones that caused her to howl like a demonic opera singer in the middle of the night, terrifying us all. One day when the Hans Christian Andersen book was gone—"lost," she said—we stopped asking for it. (Though her howling nightmares continued up until Krystal disappeared.)

Bettelheim argues that fairy tales play an essential role in child development. "The strange, most ancient, most distant, and, at the same time, most familiar locations which a fairy tale speaks about suggest a voyage into the interior of our mind, into the realms of unawareness and the unconscious." Through fairy tales, Sam and I could venture into the dark, bewitched forest from the comfort of our beds. We could imagine starvation, mutilation, even death, while our own bellies were full, our own feet attached and warm beneath the blankets. Moreover, we welcomed darkness and evil, pain and suffering. We recognized those parts within ourselves, our primal impulses lurking like wild creatures in the forest, hidden yet nonetheless present. "[A]ll the child's wishful thinking gets embodied in a good fairy," Bettelheim writes, "all his destructive wishes in an evil witch."

There is a fairy tale in the Grimms' collection that makes me think of Sam and me. It is called, simply, "Little Brother, Little Sister." In the story, an orphaned brother and sister escape the home of their evil stepmother and run away, crossing meadows, fields and stones, and arriving finally at the forest. Brother and Sister are pitiful creatures, as children in fairy tales tend to be. When it rains, Sister cries, "God and our hearts are crying together!" In the forest, the siblings find a hollow in a tree and sleep there, "tired from sorrow and hunger." Meanwhile, their evil stepmother, who is—unsurprisingly—a witch, has poisoned the water supply in the forest. Over the course of the next day, the siblings wander through the forest, hungry and parched, and yet each time they find water, Little Sister senses that something is amiss. "Don't drink," she tells her brother, and he doesn't. But at the third spring, Sister's warning comes too late. Brother drinks and is turned into a deer. Weeping, Sister fashions a collar for him from a golden garter and weaves a leash of rushes, by which she leads her deer through the forest.

Sam and I ran away from time to time, though never together. For us, "running away" meant traversing the half mile from Mom's to Dad's, or vice versa. "Running away" meant we were violating the carefully negotiated parenting agreement, triggering a deluge of phone calls to lawyers and mediators, those enigmatic figures whom I never met, but who appeared when summoned. In my mind, these people were powerful spirits, tricksters, goblins, witches. I feared and despised them.

The first time I run away, around age seven, I pack a tiny suitcase made of brightly colored vinyl. In it, I cram my favorite stuffed animal, my *Dear America* diaries, and some framed family photos. I am calm, no longer crying. The twilight air is cool and dry. I slip quietly out the front door of Dad and Krystal's house, my suitcase bumping along behind me on its miniature wheels. I head down the long, steep hill of Jamaica Way, turn right at Maplewood Lane, the left at Lima Street, and then begin the slow gradual ascent toward Orchard Road. I could travel this distance with my eyes closed. In this neighborhood, there is nothing I am afraid of, aside from my own family. All the lawns are nicely mowed, the landscaping plain and tidy. The houses are painted unobtrusive shades of beige or green or blue. All the porchlights are on; all the garage doors are closed shut. I pass nobody. I hear crickets and an occasional dog barking and the noisy grating of the suitcase wheels on smooth cement. At Mom's, I hide the suitcase in the lava rock on the side of the house before punching in the garage code and going inside.

I don't remember what happens next—whether I spend the night, or if I am returned to Dad's like a lost wallet. I don't remember why I have fled in the first place. Only the solo journey remains seared in my memory—how small I felt, yet how sure I was of my purpose.

And what if Sam had come with me? And why did I leave him behind?

I want to pause the tale of "Little Brother, Little Sister" in the forest. I want to ignore what happens next—the arrival of a king and his hunting party, a wedding and a birth, the return of the evil stepmother and her final vanquishing. If only Brother and Sister could stay in the forest, safe in their warm cottage. There they could forage for berries and mushrooms. Far away from their former lives, their bad memories could soften to warm nostalgia. They could heal. "If only the brother had had his human form, it would have been a wonderful life," the fairy tale goes. But even if their life isn't *wonderful*, it is still good. Couldn't they live forever here? Couldn't they?

According to Calvino, the power of the fairy tale exists in the story's "economy." "[E]vents," he writes, "regardless of their duration, become like points connected by straight-line segments in a zigzag fashion that suggests unceasing motion." The space between the plot points gives neurons room to zip around, making connections. Our own lives are not so tidy and one-dimensional, yet we feel compelled to shape chaos into narrative, to tease out the single golden thread woven through the tangle of yarn.

When I was in high school, my stepmother entered menopause. "I bled through my pants at work today," she told me one day, describing how she had to drive home while sitting on a towel, and that by the time she pulled into the garage, the towel was completely saturated in blood. "It's the change of life," she said. I shuddered, thinking of the towel, damp and sticky. "Change of life" was a strange way to describe what seemed like a biblical plague, the Nile River turned to blood.

Sam was changing too. He dressed only in sweatpants and hoodies, and rolled out of bed just in time to leave for the school bus. He stopped showering. Then he stopped talking. The story we were living in was getting darker by the day.

"Here comes the toddler," Krystal would say as Sam entered the room, his eyes downcast, shoulders slumped. Or when he forgot to take out the trash: "You know what you are? You're a loser." Or when he announced he was quitting football: "You're a fuck-up. A pothead. A weirdo like your mom and Cecil." Often my father chimed in: "Sit up straight, pal. Wash your greasy hair. You look like a flunky." I sat silently as Dad and Krystal drained Sam of his vitality, siphoned off his humanity. I believed that if anyone could break the enchantment, it would be me, if only he would listen.

"Why can't you just do what you're told?" I would ask Sam, over and over when we were alone. "If you just do what she says, then you won't get in trouble like this. It might not be good, but at least it will be bearable. I'll help you." If only he were more attentive to his chores, if only he showered and dressed, tucking in his shirt like Dad wanted, if only he cleaned up his room, said "good morning" in a chipper voice, then the curse would be broken. What I didn't say: *If only you could be like me.*

"I fucking hate it here, Lauren. This place is a hellhole," he would reply, pulling his hood over his eyes. "And I'm sick of taking out Krystal's disgusting bloody trash."

Years later, I would read about the effects of childhood trauma in Van der Kolk's *The Body Keeps the Score*, how when our fight or flight systems are shown not to be effective against a threat, our bodies and brains begin to shut down. We collapse, disengage from the world around us. We may even lose the ability to register physical pain. Reading the description, I see my brother's mischievous eyes turned dull and expressionless. When Krystal hurled insults at him, he didn't even flinch. He didn't respond at all. Trapped, his defenses had been unable to protect him. Later, I would learn that during those years Sam had pleaded with Mom to let him live with her, but legally, she had no power to do that. All those lawyers, psychologists, and judges had failed to protect him from his father and stepmother. I had failed to protect him. Dissociation became my brother's last defense. His brain and body had begun to shut down.

One day, looking back through my childhood journals, I discover a note in Sam's handwriting, tucked into the back pocket of a journal along with some movie ticket stubs and old photos. I immediately recognize it from the night he ran away. I hadn't thought about this night in years, but I remember it clearly.

Dad and Krystal have gone out to a concert or out with friends. For weeks now, Krystal has banned Sam from eating with the family, forbade him, in fact, from eating any food she has prepared. "Only friends of mine eat at my table," she says. As usual, Dad says nothing. They eat their chicken parmesan and drink their wine, as if this is all normal. I pretend it's normal, too. Meanwhile, Sam scavenges, subsisting on whole milk and Ritz crackers. But tonight, there is no dinner at all, no parents. The house is quiet except for the ticking of the bird clock in the kitchen. The rooms are dark. It's just the two of us. We can eat together.

I find my brother lying on his bed, staring up at the ceiling. Piles of clothes and books lie scattered around the room.

"Hey," I say.

"Hey," he responds, not looking up.

"I'll make dinner if you do the dishes." He sits up and glares at me.

"Thanks but no thanks. I'm treated like a dog here," he says. "I'm going to Mom's. To eat actual food." I watch as he begins stuffing things into his backpack: a geometry textbook, binders with their pages flying loose.

"It's not Mom's night," I say, stating the obvious.

"So?"

I don't try to stop him, don't offer to go with him. I had decided long ago that I would follow the rules, bide my time, find refuge in my journals and books, in the hidden place deep inside myself. I watch as Sam walks out the front door, slams it behind him. He disappears down the front steps, his silhouette illuminated by lamplight, then gone. The night is cold, and the moon shines like a flashlight in the cloudless sky. I close my eyes, and with him I travel the long, steep hill down Jamaica Way, the right turn at Maplewood Lane, the left at Lima Street, and the slow gradual ascent toward Orchard Road. I loop my arm through his. I tell him that I will always be by his side, always. That we are together in this still, dark world. That here, in this in-between place is the entire universe, a story for the ages. It is ours to take.

I open my eyes, and I'm alone.

The house is like a tomb. I turn on the stove, boil some water, make myself a box of macaroni. I wash and dry my dishes, spray down the countertops, sweep the floors. Everything must be spotless. On my way back to my bedroom, I stop first at Sam's. A scrap of folded paper lies on his bed. On the outside, he's written in pencil, "I'm at Mom's." I unfold it to read the inside: "I'M SICK OF BEING TREATED LIKE

A DOG. p.s. Lauren can do the bathrooms." I tuck the note inside my journal, feeling like the only person in the world.

A few years later, I would write in my journal: *Things change so—suddenly. Or maybe they change gradually, but we just don't realize what has happened until the moment hits us.* But the fairy tale always begins at the precise moment of action. Years turn to minutes, and seconds last a lifetime. Almost three decades ago, I held a blue bubblegum cigar in my hands. My brother wailed. My mother fed him. I blinked and here I am, no longer biding my time, on the brink now of giving birth to my first child, a new generation.

Taped to the wall behind my computer is my favorite photo of Sam and me, aged two and five. It was taken, I believe, in my preschool classroom. Seeing it every day makes me feel closer to my brother—no longer little—who lives in New England, a world away from my home in Mississippi. In the photo, our arms are wrapped around each other; our affection is palpable. We are grinning wildly, dressed in oversized, primary-colored clothes.

Looking at this photo, I can't help but think we were as charmed and innocent as the children in fairy tales, our heads round as cabbages, our faces vulnerable and open. *Little brother, little sister.* What tenderness I feel for these two who, even in the enchanted forest, found a home in one another.

Parenting Diary: Winter Wonderland

December 31, 2000—Lauren called me at 7:45 a.m. from her Dad's house. She said, "I'm sorry this is such short notice, Mom, but Sam and I will be staying at Dad's house for New Year's Eve and New Year's Day. We'll see you on Tuesday after school. I've never spent New Year's Eve with my dad before so it is only fair that I stay here this year." I said, "No, Lauren, you have to come home. We have all kinds of things planned. I want you to come home." Lauren said, "No, I'm not. I'm going to stay at my Dad's house because I love him and miss him." (She had been at his house for eight days). I said, "No, Lauren. You need to come home. Can I talk to Sam?" Lauren said, "Sam is sleeping right now." I said, "Lauren, I'll expect you home at 8 a.m." Lauren said, "No. That is not what I want to do," and hung up on me. We had been invited to Cecil's dad's house for a brunch and at night had plans to go to Skate the Lake in Evergreen. Cecil and I had driven to Evergreen and had bought the tickets the day before.

I was shocked and felt physically ill. The children did not arrive home. I tried calling Matt's house. The phone rang with no pick-up by the answering machine. The emotional pain was intense and I couldn't stop crying. I went to my health club and worked out and came home and took a long shower and decided that I was not going to go under emotionally on this. Cecil and I went out to dinner and decided that on Tuesday, January 2, I would call Howard and have him file a contempt of court citation against Matt for blocking access to the children on my visitation days. I did not call on Monday, January 1 because I didn't think I could deal with another rejection by my child.

Happy New Year's Eve. My hands are colder than they've ever been. My fingers are so numb, I think they might fall off. All around us: snow. Heavy snow, clumped on the branches of pine trees, weighing down the saplings until their tops arch toward the ground like acrobats. Snow so deep, it could swallow you whole. Snow like quicksand. The only sounds in the forest are the *crunch crunch* of our snowshoes, and the *whoosh* of our snow pants, and the occasional *plop* of snow falling from a tree branch. I think this must be what Edmund saw when he tumbled out of the coat closet and into the wintry forest of Narnia. Beauty. Stillness. Piercing cold. I half expect to see a faun appear from behind the trunk of a pine, or the White Witch's sleigh, gliding down the trail ahead of us. (Oh, I could go for some hot chocolate and Turkish delight right now.) But the forest is silent aside from the sounds of us.

Crunch crunch whoosh whoosh plop. I squeeze my mitten-covered hands in rhythm, alternating one after the other. It hurts to squeeze. My fingers are stiff, but I know I need to keep the blood flowing to them. *Crunch crunch* squeeze. *Crunch crunch* squeeze. Ahead of me, my stepmother's yellow ski jacket bobs up and down, setting the pace. I know Sam is behind me, my father in the rear. We are quiet now as we make our final descent to the parking lot. *What if we don't make it? What if we have to sleep in the forest?* The sun sinks to the edge of the horizon, and the shadows of the trees deepen to blue.

This morning, when I called to tell my mother I would be staying at Dad's, her voice sounded ragged and desperate. *I want you to come home.* The voice of someone who is clinging by their fingers to the edge of a cliff. That's what I pictured: my mother clinging to the edge of the cliff, while I watched, my feet planted on the ground. *No,* I said firmly. My stepmother listened, sipping her coffee. Sausage sizzled in a pan on the stove, and the smell of Pillsbury biscuits wafted from the oven. *I don't want to*, I said, and my mother's fingers slipped, and I hung up the phone.

There, there's the car. Sweet relief to see the old champagne-colored Cadillac that my father bought from his new father-in-law. He calls it *the boat.* I keep squeezing my fingers, even as I remove my snowshoes, shake the snow free from their metal spikes before setting them in the trunk. In the plush, velvety back seat of the car, the blood slowly returns to my fingertips. The blood feels like burning. *Should we stop for hot chocolate on the way home?* my stepmother asks, turning to look at us from the front passenger seat. Sam and I squeal with pleasure. *Yes!* Our cheeks are rosy, cherubic. She rests her hand on my father's thigh. Outside, the shadows of trees blur into a mass of inky black as we make our descent to the city, its lights twinkling in the distance.

Discernment

You are lying on your bed at Mom's, belly down on the white comforter with pink rosettes, feet in the air, listening to the new Paul Simon album on your stereo and thinking about baptism. You fell in love with Simon & Garfunkel when you were thirteen, on a trip to Maine with Aunt Esther. The trip was her bat mitzvah present to you, and the two of you drove through the winding, wooded roads of Acadia National Park, pausing to toss a Frisbee when a beach appeared through the trees, listening to Tracy Chapman, TLC, and Simon & Garfunkel on the car's tape player. You belted out the words to "Cecilia," not totally understanding what they meant, not caring. The songs from *Bridge Over Troubled Water* remind you of your aunt, of the faraway place where forest meets ocean, where the world is muted in grays and blues and greens.

From Simon & Garfunkel, you discovered Paul Simon's solo albums. You don't mind being the only one in your friend group who loves Simon's music, the only one who bought his new CD *Surprise* when it peeked out from the alphabetized CD rack at Best Buy. Doesn't matter that he is "old" now. You like old music, music with a story and a message and a meaning. It's something you and Chris—the boy you love who may or may not love you back—have in common, priding yourselves on listening to *good* music—Charles Mingus, Dave Brubeck, Pat Metheney. You really *listen* to the cadence, the rhythm, the unexpected melody. You are musicians. You play piano in Jazz Band A.

He plays snare on the drumline. And now you both are in Percussion Ensemble, though Chris is admittedly more dedicated and talented. These are all topics you could discuss if you were to ever go on a date.

You study Simon's CD insert; the cover art is a close-up photo of a baby's face, her eyes wide, cheeks smooth and round, a button nose. A fresh baby, filled with curiosity and surprise. Isn't this what you long for? Freshness and newness? Innocence? This is what baptism will be like—you will be a blank slate, wiped clean of sin. A fresh vessel ready to accept God's love. In your Rite of Christian Initiation of Adults classes, you've learned that there are *candidates* and *catechumens*. All of you are trying to become Catholic, but the candidates have already been baptized in a different Christian faith. You are one of the few catechumens, one of the unbaptized ones. You are also the youngest person in the RCIA class. And the only Jew.

Part of you is glad that you were never baptized as a baby, that your Catholic father never insisted on it, because now you can understand and appreciate what you are doing. There will be a *before* and an *after*. This is the before—sticky, full of desire and doubt. The after will be clean and pure.

Already, after listening on repeat, you know the lyrics to the first track of the CD by heart. The song is about the questions most people ask others but not themselves—why do you live where you do? Why do you believe what you believe? In this way, you're different: you ask yourself these questions all the time. How can you be a Catholic? A Jew? Simon sings against a smattering of drums and synth. *How can you?*

You like the earnestness of his voice, the imperfections in it. The lack of accusation. *We all have an inner voice*, he sings, *no matter your religion*. A beat of silence before the electric guitar chords ripple.

Your own inner voice is incessant, full of contradictions. Listen closely. Open your heart to the sacraments, it says. Or is that God's voice? And what about Chris? Is God telling you to open your heart to him, too? You imagine what it would be like to touch Chris's cheek, to brush your fingertips against the little blond curls on his neck.

We seek infinite light, and yet we sleep in the dark, Simon sings, his voice trailing off. This is what you want: *Infinite light. Infinite love.* Catholicism makes these promises. Ignore the part about sleeping in the dark.

RCIA classes take place after Sunday morning mass in the St. Thomas More Church basement. You go to church now even on the weekends when you are with Mom. You can drive yourself. You have your own car—Krystal's old Volvo—and you are seventeen. One year away from being in charge of your own life.

Mom is in her pajamas—baggy sweatpants and one of Cecil's old T-shirts—and cradling a cup of coffee when you come down the stairs in the morning. You are in church clothes.

"You want something to eat? Toaster strudel?" she asks.

"I'm okay. I'll eat after mass," you reply. You don't tell her that you are not supposed to eat for two hours before you take communion, that your stomach is supposed to be empty to receive Christ's Body and Blood. That you can't take communion yet, but you are practicing. That your stomach is empty in solidarity. That the emptiness feels holy.

Your mom is quiet, as if your rejection of the toaster strudel is yet another rejection of her. Disappointment fills the room like a thick, choking fog. A month ago, when you told her you would be converting to Catholicism, it was like a dam inside her cracked, her anger and sadness spilling forth into desperation. "Why?" she kept asking. "Why are you doing this? Are *they* telling you to do this?"

"I'm doing this because *I* want to do this, because this is what I believe now," you said calmly, firmly.

"You're turning your back on your heritage. Your family. All the people who helped you with your bat mitzvah."

"I'm not turning my back on anybody. I'm still here, aren't I?"

But you often think of your Aunt Hedy, who taught you how to read the Torah, and a pang of guilt hits you, knowing how disappointed she must be. It's a kind of open secret, what you're doing in the basement of the church, and you can feel your Jewish family's scorn—or is it pity? Unnerving, distracting. Threatening to derail your mission.

Mom's question continues to echo around your thoughts, even now that you have reached a kind of silent equilibrium. *Why? Why are you doing this?* Maybe part of you wants to become Catholic because it pleases your dad and Krystal, because they hated that you were (are) Jewish, and so a part of you began to hate it, too. But even so, this is no longer a question of pleasing parents, but a question of faith and belief. *Infinite light.* Questionable motivations can still lead to good and holy outcomes.

Sometimes you hear Cecil talking to your mom behind the closed door of their bedroom. "Sara, it's going to be fine. Wait a year, maybe two. She's going through a phase. No way is this going to stick."

A *phase*? Not a phase. This is you, your new life.

"Discernment" is the focus of today's RCIA class, which is led by a nun, Sister Felicia. You're surprised to see that Sister Felicia isn't wearing robes and a habit like the nuns in movies, but rather a pink wool sweater, her gray hair cropped into a short, practical cut. She could be somebody's grandmother—if she wasn't a nun.

Discernment, she says, is a way of opening yourself up to God's will, of allowing God to show you your path forward. Discernment is not magic or fortune-telling. It does not involve talking or asking, reason or logic. It is simply a form of listening, of becoming neutral. This is what St. Ignatius called a "Holy Indifference," a detachment from the material world, in order to serve and praise God. Once you allow yourself to do what God is asking you to do, a sense of calm and tranquility enters your life.

You listen to Sister Felicia, rapt. She exudes a sense of quiet peace; everyone in the room is mesmerized by her presence, including Hilda, your RCIA sponsor, who is taking notes, her shiny red lips pursed in concentration. Detachment, tranquility. For years you have been untangling desires—your own and your parents'—but what if you could just listen to God instead, and do what He wants you to do? Remember Jeremiah from your bat mitzvah haftarah portion. The prophet Jeremiah says to God: "I don't know how to speak, for I am a youth." And God tells him not to worry, that "wherever I will send you, you will go, and whatever I will command you, you will speak."

If only God's voice could be that clear, commanding. If only the voices in your mind could quiet themselves long enough to listen.

After the class, Hilda says she wants you to talk to Sister Felicia with her. She is looking at you with what can only be called compassion. As if she is really trying to see you, *you* the aspiring Catholic. Hilda, whose lipstick is always endearingly smeared, her mascara applied a little too thick, her teased-out hair too hair-sprayed. Hilda is one of Krystal's few friends who is approachable, genuinely good and generous. Her son Taylor, a large and affable boy, played on Sam's football team. Faith seems to come naturally to her, and you sometimes wonder if this grace is only available to those who were born into the Catholic Church, who can speak it like a first language.

You follow Hilda to the front of the room, where she introduces the two of you to Sister Felicia. "Lauren is only seventeen, and has decided to become a Catholic," Hilda explains, "which is very brave and self-aware. Her mother is Jewish, and she was raised in the Jewish faith."

Sister Felicia studies you a moment before speaking. "You know, Jesus himself was never a Christian," she says, a twinkle in her eye. "And you should always respect your Jewish roots. You should always respect your mother."

"Okay," you say. "I will. I do."

But you're not thinking of your mother or your Jewish roots as you sit at your desk writing in your notebook that evening. You're thinking of Chris. You keep replaying the conversation the two of you had in the band room before school let out last week. Had he been flirting with you? Or was he just being his usual friendly self? Your pen hovers over the notebook's pages, unwilling to commit an answer to paper. *Can I discern if I should pursue a relationship with him?* You write. *Or, is that too trivial?*

It's your friend Shayna's idea to go swing dancing at The Mercury Café. She proposes the plan to the rest of your unofficial study group—you, Chris, and Teddy—during first period while you sit in the library finishing homework. It is a given that you will be on board. You always go along with Shayna's plans. She is the boldest member in your group of somewhat nerdy high achievers. She wears crop tops paired with flowy purple skirts, sings opera, and is the only person you know who chooses not to eat gluten for health reasons. You met five years ago when you were both studying for your bat mitzvah. She knows you're becoming a Catholic now, but hasn't offered any judgments or asked many questions. You are grateful for this.

"Chris, can you drive?" she asks, and gives you a subtle eyebrow raise. "You have the cleanest car."

"Sure," Chris says. "I like swing dancing. And swing music."

"Theodore?" you say, looking at your friend Teddy, who Shayna happens to have a crush on.

"Why not?" Teddy says. "But you should know I'm a horrible dancer."

The Mercury Café is in downtown Denver, a world away from the green lawns and cul-de-sacs of your suburb. A light snow has begun to fall, and Chris drives slowly and carefully, properly signaling and checking his mirrors, following the directions that Shayna reads off to him from her printed MapQuest directions even as you get to the confusing one-way streets of the city.

"Chris, you kind of drive like a grandma," Shayna says, playfully.

"You really do, Chris," you say. "Look! Everyone is passing us."

"Chris, *thank you* for following the laws, despite the maniacs in the back seat," Teddy says, and Chris's cheeks turn rosy. He looks handsome in his wool peacoat, the nice one he wears to orchestra and band concerts.

Walking inside The Mercury Café is like entering a fortune-teller's den. The walls are painted a rich crimson; strings of lights hang from the ceilings, woven among garlands and big, shiny Christmas ornaments. The dance floor is upstairs, and the dancing has already started, big band swing music pumping from the speakers around the room. A line of women stands on one side, facing a line of men. You stand across from Chris, but then the lines rotate and you are stuck with a stranger, a middle-aged man with slicked-back hair. This was not the plan.

Slow . . . slow . . . quick quick . . . slow . . . slow . . . quick quick. And now the collegiate shag!

You look over at Shayna and give her your best *what-the-hell-is-happening* look. She's dancing with a sweaty, balding man. She shrugs at you, smiles politely at the man, keeps dancing.

"Partner change!" the swing teacher yells. Your new partner looks like Jack Nicholson in *As Good as It Gets*. "Gird up your loins!" he says to you, smiling broadly and offering you his arm, but before you can find out what that means, you say "excuse me," and grab Chris's hand.

"I'm not dancing with any more creepy old dudes," you say, holding onto him. He laughs.

"I think that's wise." His hands are warm but not sweaty—snare drum-playing hands. He's a pretty good dancer, has no trouble following the *slow slow quick quick* instructions, and soon he leads you spinning around the dance floor.

"Glenn Miller Orchestra," he says, cocking his head to listen to the music.

"'In the Mood,'" you respond, and your heart skips a beat. "We played this in Jazz Band."

What if you leaned in and kissed him now? But you know, even as you ask yourself the question, that you won't. Not here, where your insides feel as warm as the light glinting off the ornaments, the heat from bodies moving around the room. You imagine seeing yourself as Chris sees you now, in your boot cut jeans and most flattering sweater, the one you picked out with Mom on a shopping trip to Nordstrom Rack. Your naturally curly hair, now blow-dried and straightened. Does he think you're pretty? Has he examined your face the way you've examined his? You like the way his lower lip sort of pouts out when he's focused, the way that he keeps Chapstick in his pocket and applies it every so often, the beginnings of blond stubble along his otherwise smooth jaw line, his pale blue eyes.

Chris isn't like the other boys you've liked—sometimes he dresses like a Sunday school teacher, in checkered shirts and brown leather shoes. And he's never looked at you in that eager way of boys you've dated in the past. But you are attracted to his innocence, his harmlessness. Either he's too shy to make a move, or he only likes you as a friend. Impossible to discern what to do with your burning feelings other than pour them into your notebook.

This is the way it is with God, too. A constant show of love and devotion and faith in exchange for—a promise, a mystery. Infinite light.

"We don't ask God to send us signs," Father Andrew said last week during the homily. "God doesn't appear just because we want Him to. When Thomas doubted the resurrection, Jesus appeared to him, asked Thomas to touch his wounds. He said: blessed are they who have not seen, and yet have believed. Jesus is saying that because you asked for proof, you are missing the miracle, the mystery of faith. What miracle are you missing right now in your own life?"

But Jesus still appeared to Thomas, you wanted to say. Why did he appear to Thomas if he didn't have to? You've never asked for signs, though you've secretly hoped for one. All you want is a small thing, a tiny found object, the brush of a warm hand, something that would let you know: you are on the right path. But all you have now is mystery, no resolution.

The song ends, and the swing instructor thanks everyone for coming, and you squeeze Chris's arm and say, "That was fun, I'm glad we danced together," and he says, "Me too." You find Shayna and Teddy, who also ended up dancing together, and tell them all about the old guy who told you to "gird your loins," and how Chris saved you. (Or did you save yourself?) And you bask in the music and the dusky glow of The Mercury Café and your funny friends, your ability to make them laugh, and this feeling of lightness follows you out into the snow which has begun to gather in cottony drifts, and past the shadowy outlines of skyscrapers, and you're floating along the quiet highway in Chris's clean car, back to the suburbs.

And now you are alone. Crying, perhaps overdramatically, in the girl's bathroom next to the band room. You study your tear-streaked face in the mirror with distant curiosity. Like the face belongs to a stranger. The eyelashes in wet clumps, the red and blotchy cheeks, fat quivering lips.

For once, though, you are not crying because of boys or because you have disappointed your parents in some new way. You are crying because you have been kicked out of Percussion Ensemble. When you told your band teacher—your favorite teacher—that you would be getting initiated into your church the same night as the Percussion Ensemble's regional competition finals, and that you wouldn't be able to go, his features hardened, and he told you that if you can't compete, then you can't practice. And that's that. And you realize you had been working and practicing toward the regional competition finals in Percussion Ensemble as diligently as you had been studying to become a Catholic. Practicing scales on the marimba during your off periods at school, humming your parts to yourself in the car, in the shower. Your stomach is clenched like a fist. No more practicing with Chris and your band friends every Tuesday and Thursday after school. No more satisfaction from a well-executed run, your mallets—two in each hand, like an extension of your fingers—flying across the marimba. Your presence there now would only be a hindrance to the team.

But there's something about that face in the mirror, something alluring about her pain. It's the pain of a martyr, of someone who chooses faith and duty over pleasure and camaraderie. And when compared with crucifixion, this pain is bearable. And not just bearable, but desirable. You think about the man in your RCIA class who said that he puts a pebble in his shoe every day during Lent, because the constant discomfort is a reminder of Jesus's sacrifice. And maybe this is your pebble, your reminder that faith comes with an earthly cost.

"Buck up," you tell the mirror. "You're okay." The same way your father says it. You splash cool water on your face, dry it with a stiff paper towel from the dispenser. If you walk quickly, you'll make it to class on time.

On a Saturday in March, you stop by Chris's house. The two of you are going to see a documentary about Hurricane Katrina and the Louisiana Bayou at the natural history museum downtown. A date. But not a date. But it could be. Snow is falling again, a melty spring snow. The flakes are wet and heavy; the streets turn to gray slush.

Chris's house is in a suburb like yours, only nicer. You ring the doorbell, and a gray-haired man with a kind smile and the same blue eyes as Chris opens the door, tells you he's Chris's grandfather. The man asks you about colleges and you tell him you're going in-state, to the University of Colorado. You just found out that you got into the honors program with scholarships. "Nothing wrong with that," he says, as if maybe there is.

At the museum, the din of voices echoes off the stone floors, and the huge glass windows of the atrium reveal the gray-white sky. After the film ends, you and Chris wander around for hours. First the Botswana dioramas. Cheetahs frozen mid-pounce. Wax human figures with painted faces in grass skirts. You tell Chris about the time your family slept over at the museum as part of some family night for members. Mom's idea, of course, but then she couldn't fall asleep because a man in the adjacent exhibit snored all night.

You tell him that you remember lying on the floor in your sleeping bag, hearing the sounds of all the people settling in, first hushed voices and then the rhythms of their breathing. The lights were turned off in the dioramas then, but you could still sense the animals in their cases watching you.

"That's a little creepy," Chris says. The two of you are walking through the Benjamin Franklin exhibit now, pausing every so often to read or look at an interesting display. But mostly talking.

"Yeah, I guess so, but it felt more like they were protecting me, than ready to pounce," you say, thinking of that night. And of all the times you've come to this museum before. When you were little, you lived in a house down the street, and your mom would take you and Sam here all the time. You could walk those few blocks in the cool shade of the trees that lined Montview Boulevard. Those memories are scenes frozen in time now. The little girl you once were is like a fondly remembered childhood friend, like a character in a favorite book, her image fading with time. You wonder if this moment with Chris will ever become one of those memories—distant and belonging almost to someone else. Paused in time and space like the gazelles in the diorama, forever grazing in a fake savanna. You wouldn't mind being frozen in time with Chris before the two of you go your separate ways to college—Chris to a private college in upstate New York, you to the public university just an hour away.

"Do you ever wish you could go back to being a kid?" you ask.

"Technically, we're still kids," he replies. You give him a light push. He laughs and pretends to stagger.

"Yeah, for like another month," you say. "You know what I mean. Like if you could go back to simpler times, a more innocent place. Would you do it?" He puts his hand to his chin, a pensive gesture which reminds you of the way your dad strokes his mustache when he reads the newspaper.

"No, I don't think so," he finally says. "I'm too excited to see what's next. I want to go to college, learn new things. See a different place. Discover who I am."

"You mean Shayna telling you your Enneagram number wasn't enough of a discovery for you?"

He grins. "Wow, how could I forget? Yeah, no. I'm not convinced that stuff is real."

You don't tell him that Shayna's assessment of you as The Peacemaker ("because you're always trying to keep the peace between your parents, because you hate conflict and disagreement") has continued to haunt you. You can't tell if she's right, if this is who you are, or simply who you have been forced to be.

The nice thing about a museum date is that when conversation dwindles, there is always something to look at, to draw in the eye. You make a loop around the upper atrium, gazing down at the giant skeleton of a brontosaurus, then get chili and cornbread from the T-Rex Café. You are hoping for something, the brush of his fingers against yours, a meaningful look, a confession. You imagine him in New York, walking through a snowy campus in his peacoat and wool hat. "I'll miss you," you want to say, but don't.

When you get back to Chris's house, the snow has stopped but the sky is still a murky gray, growing darker as daylight wanes. The two of you sit in awkward silence in the idling car. You look at Chris's face and then at his house. Maybe his grandfather is watching from a window you can't see. Your palms feel clammy. Your heart is pounding in your chest. Every sound is magnified in this silence—the low rumble of the car, the whoosh of the heat through the vents. And then Chris leans forward—*finally*—only not for a kiss, but a hug. A warm, simple hug.

Spring break is cold and blustery, and you are at your dad's house. Your last spring break of high school. Nothing is planned this year—no family vacation, no special outings. The goal is simply to get through. A thin dusting of snow covers the crocuses and early daffodil shoots that have begun to sprout in Krystal's garden. The tension in the air is palpable, erratic as the weather. Krystal is at Sam's throat, pointing out everything he's doing wrong. Earlier this year, he carved "FUCK YOU" into his bedroom wall with a pocketknife, and she went ballistic and bagged all his stuff into trash bags and set them on the curb. You pray for God to make your brother want to do his chores, to obey like you do, to let her insults shed like water off his back.

Remember after your bat mitzvah, when she called you "the Jewish Princess," like it was a curse? *And you felt cursed.*

When she forbade you from going to mass with the family because you were Jewish now—as if you hadn't always been Jewish—and you made up your own makeshift church service alone in your room? *You had never felt more alone.*

When she bought you a cheap menorah and made you light the candles by yourself, as a punishment? *That menorah still lives in the basement pantry, like a phantom. You see it whenever you go down to fetch a can of tomatoes, a jar of jelly.*

Look at you now. You are better at her religion than she is. You are a kinder, more righteous person. At night you say a rosary and pray for God to soften her heart, to help her forgive. Just as you have forgiven. Like a real Christian.

This is the year you learn that the Last Supper was a Passover Seder. And what a revelation this is: Jesus at a Passover Seder, breaking the unleavened bread and eating bitter herbs, reclining, asking the question of *why on this night*, recounting the Exodus. Did one of the disciples slaughter a paschal lamb for the seder, just as each year your family places a symbolic roasted shank bone on the seder plate?

Oh, so this is why in church they say that Jesus *is* the paschal lamb. He is the sacrifice. *Paschal* and *Pesach*, the same root. *Pesach*, Hebrew for Passover. The enslaved Jews in Egypt put lamb's blood on the lintels of their doors, and the Angel of Death *passed over* their houses. Now you understand why Passover and Easter are always so close together, why your parents' custody schedule gets so complex in the spring—the fighting over who gets Spring Break, and what if it overlaps with Passover, and Passover always overlapping somehow with Easter.

This year, Passover starts on a Monday evening, the Monday of Holy Week, five days before Holy Saturday when you will receive the sacraments of baptism, first communion, and confirmation. (And you haven't forgotten the Percussion Ensemble competition.)

Sister Felicia said Jesus was never Christian. Perhaps she meant that you can still partake in the seder, that you don't have to worry so much about breaking rules. Since you have proclaimed your intention to become Catholic, you have felt God looking over your shoulder like a holy scorekeeper. All your life you have felt as if you were doing religion wrong, rooting for two opposing teams. Even now that you have chosen your team, you still feel inadequate. And so, you have stopped participating in the Shabbat prayers, to your mother's grave disappointment. You stand there, mute, while your family does the blessing, their voices off-key as always. You do not even cover your eyes with your hands, or bow your head. Instead you look straight into the candles' flames. You have stopped saying Hebrew words altogether, as though Jesus might hear you and not recognize you as one of his flock.

But Jesus was never Christian. And Passover is your favorite holiday; you can admit that to yourself. The holiday where your eccentric grandfather, himself the son of a rabbi (grandson of a rabbi, too), leads a theatrical family reenactment of the Exodus, when you eat your mother's matzah ball soup, and make Hillel sandwiches with *matzah*, *charoset*, and *maror*. And you and Sam make a plot to steal the *afikomen* when Poppi isn't looking and hide it in a sock drawer. When you read that Annie Dillard quote from the family Haggadah after dipping greens into salt water: *If I swallowed a seed and some soil, could I grow grapes in my mouth . . . Why leap ye, ye high hills?* And you allow yourself to sink into the familiarity of your heritage. *Respect your mother. Respect your Jewish roots.* And what is the line between respect and worship?

You: the bridge between Old Testament and New.

Your silent prayer: *Please, let me be with Jesus, as though this seder were the Last Supper.*

When you enter St. Thomas More for the Easter Vigil, the lights are dimmed, and the giant crucifix above the altar is draped in a white sheet. You think (as you will write later in your notebook), that Jesus looks enormous and triumphant. You feel small. You are wearing a cream-colored dress flecked with gold, that Krystal plucked from the racks of TJ Maxx. All the candidates and catechumens are also dressed in white. They are here with their husbands and wives, or their fiancées. Most of them are converting for their Catholic partners.

You meet first in the church basement, where you have met every Sunday for the past nine months. The RCIA coordinator drapes the candidates and catechumens in a synthetic white fabric. *To protect your clothes from the water and oil,* she says. You finger the cheap, shiny material, disappointed that the smocks are not made of something more natural, like linen or cotton. She then hands out stubby white candles, the same kind of plain Shabbat candles you can find in the kosher section at the grocery store, wrapped in a paper collar so the wax won't drip onto your hands. She lights one, and you pass the flame from one candle to the next, and no one speaks as you walk down the aisle in a line—like penitents, or ghosts, faces illuminated by the glow.

Fire is powerful and transformative. This is why Jews hold their fingernails up to the light of the braided Havdalah candle, to see the reflection and flicker of the flame on their own bodies. *Baruch atah*

Adonai Eloheinu melech ha'olam, bo're m'orei ha'esh. Blessed are You our God, Creator of the universe, who creates the lights of the fire. Even your candles, small and cheap, seem to convey the gravity of this evening. The holiness.

You sit next to Hilda, who smells of hairspray and floral perfume, her bright red lipstick slightly smeared in the corners of her mouth. Dad and Krystal are a few rows back. Sam is with Mom and Cecil tonight, and they are not here. You did not invite them, knowing Mom wouldn't want to come. She's always thought Catholicism was gruesome, gory. Plus, watching you genuflect and make the sign of the cross would be like rubbing salt in her wound. Her absence is a small mercy.

Does the ritual matter more than the becoming? This is your silent question, as the deacon anoints your forehead with scented oil and water. As the wafer meets your tongue. *Don't chew*, you have been instructed. *This is Christ's body, transubstantiated.*

Father Andrew told your RCIA class that sometimes Satanists steal the blessed host, and that once he chased one of these Satanists down. He offered this story as proof. If the Satanists go to such lengths to steal these wafers, then the wafers must actually be Christ's body. You've never seen a Satanist, but you imagine they might look something like the goth kids at your school? Tackled by a priest in green robes. You couldn't help but smile.

The wafer is Christ's body; the wine is His blood. But the body tastes like rice paper and the blood tastes like Manischewitz. Such is the mystery of faith.

Later, when it is all over, you will wonder why you felt more Catholic before your initiation than you do now. Have you really been scrubbed clean from the inside out? Perhaps it is this sense of fleeting purity, cleanness in the metaphorical eyes of God, or perhaps it is that your brain is filled with more earthly and eternal questions than it can possibly hold, that you decide to write Chris an old-fashioned letter.

Because here is one mystery you think you can solve, the mystery of his feelings for you.

Dear Chris,

Have you been to Yellowstone? My mom and stepdad took us there once on a family vacation. And there were these pools of clear blue water, bluer than the water in a pool. If you didn't know better, you'd think they were icy cold. But if you jumped in, you'd be boiled alive. That's how I feel. Placid, but boiling over inside.

You stare at the page, imagining him reading these words. The metaphor is too much. What are you trying to say? You crumple up the paper and try again.

Dear Chris,

If you are reading this letter, it means I've gone crazy and decided to reveal my deepest thoughts and feelings, the things that rarely escape the pages of my notebook.

But you're not crazy—you're in love. At the very least, you have discerned this. You feel detached, tranquil, just as Sister Felicia said you would. You start over on a fresh sheet of paper.

Dear Chris,

You probably don't think of yourself as mysterious, but that's how I feel about your feelings about me. Sometimes, I have an urge to kiss you, like when you laugh and your eyes crinkle up, and we're in the car, driving in bad weather. But mostly, I just want to be near you. Do you feel the same way? Here is my favorite quote. It's by Gertrude Stein. "There ain't no answer. There ain't going to be any answer. There never has been an answer. That's the answer." I am always looking for an answer, and there isn't one. But I keep looking. Because otherwise, what's the point?

All you want is the truth, distilled. Even if it hurts. You will give Chris the letter, because how can you not? You yourself have said there is no answer, yet here you are demanding one. Demanding proof, demanding a sign, demanding something you can hold on to. You might as well be writing a letter to God.

Parenting Diary: Fish Tank

JANUARY 16, 2001—I came home from work at about 5:15 p.m. and Cecil looked very upset. After I talked with Cecil, I went to Lauren's room and she was sleeping on her bed with her coat on. I let her sleep until 5:45 p.m. (She was supposed to go to her piano lesson at 6 p.m.) and then woke her up to talk to her. I gave her some hugs and kisses and asked her what happened.

Lauren told me that she went to her dad's house after school because she missed him. I asked her if her dad was normally at home at 2:40 in the afternoon. She said no, he wasn't there today, but he had been there other times. She confirmed that she did this last week, and he was at the house with Krystal and had coffee with her when she got there after school. I asked her if she had planned this with them. She said no. I explained that I was very disappointed that she had lied to Cecil and me, and that she had broken our trust. I asked her if Krystal came to her school to have lunch with her. She said, Yes, Krystal came to the school and had lunch with her when she forgot her music books, and Krystal would come to school to give them to her. I reminded Lauren that I had bought double copies of her music books, and she was supposed to leave one copy at her dad's so she wouldn't have to carry them back and forth. Lauren didn't say anything.

I asked Lauren to tell me how she was feeling and what was going on. She said nothing is going on, she just misses her dad. She then started crying, and said Cecil told her this was killing me and she didn't want me to die. I told her what he said was a figure of speech. He was worried about me because *this whole situation was causing me emotional distress. I told her not to lie to Cecil and me anymore, and to make sure that she is not deceitful in her relationship with us and other people. Lauren then cried a little and told me she felt sick and shaky. I took her temperature, and she was running a low-grade fever. I gave her some Motrin, and told her to just rest and read her book for a while. She was very listless for most of the night, although she did come downstairs and play piano and have some dessert with Sam and Cecil and me. The next day, I let her sleep in, and took her to school late. She did not want to go to school, but I didn't think she was sick. She appears to me to have the beginning signs of depression.*

No reason to go under the comforter—the white one with pink flowers—when you have a ski jacket. I lie in hibernation, wrapped in my waterproof cocoon, knees curled to my chest. Winter shadows lengthen on the wall, then disappear. Through the window, I can see the roof of the neighbor's house, the skeleton of their poplar tree. My eyelids are heavy. I feel small but dense, like an asteroid. I am hurtling through space, burning through the atmosphere. The coat is warm, and I am tired. Time to sleep.

When I wake, Mom's face hovers above me; her eyebrows knit in concern. Her cool hand presses gently against my forehead. She smells like cinnamon gum, winter air, and cigarette smoke. I love her, but I am afraid of loving her too much, or not enough. Afraid that I can hurt her, that I have already cut her to the bone.

My room is dark now except for the blue glow of the fish tank. How long have I been asleep? From where I lie, I can see the plecostomus, mouth suctioned to the glass. The black mollies dart back and forth, in and out of the plastic castle, around the fake seaweed. I am indifferent to my fish, uncaring. I forget to sprinkle their smelly fish flakes in the morning before I leave for school, but Cecil always remembers to feed them when he gets home. If they depended only on me, they'd be dead. I tell Mom I don't feel good. She takes my coat, covers me with the comforter. I hear her footsteps on the stairs, muffled voices, the canned laughter of *Everybody Loves Raymond*, the dull clang of pots on the stove. I close my eyes against the fish tank's glow and let the heaviness take me.

Ghost Family

"**W**ant to see a ghost?" the subject line of the email reads. Beth, my former stepmother's sister-in-law, has found me on the internet. She saw a viral tweet of mine, then found my website, then my email. We've been corresponding for a couple weeks now. I haven't seen Beth since I was a teenager, since the Christmas before Krystal left. Mostly, I remember Beth seated on our antique love seat doing the *New York Times* crossword puzzle in ballpoint pen, her thick blonde hair brushed back from her face while Krystal huffed, annoyed that she wasn't helping out in the kitchen.

When Beth's first email came, the phrase "the enemy of my enemy is my friend" popped into my head. A bit melodramatic, but the sentiment felt true. Krystal was the closest thing I had to an enemy, and she had hated Beth. The reason she *said* she hated her was because Beth was an atheist, and Krystal wouldn't tolerate anyone who snubbed Jesus Christ. But I knew what she really hated was that Beth was naturally blonde, had a successful career in marketing, and could play Chopin on the piano. Maybe she also hated that Beth had been born and raised an Orthodox Jew.

Perhaps all these years later, despite being married to Krystal's brother Dave, Beth and I would get along just fine. Perhaps Beth could give me answers.

Want to see a ghost? I open the email. There is a single image: a screenshot of a Google Maps street view. I recognize the house and the street immediately: a low-slung white stucco ranch with brown trim, a neatly kept lawn, and a large linden tree shading the driveway. This is the house where my stepmother grew up, where her parents lived until they died. Phyllis first in 2001, Leo in 2013. This is Cañon City, a prison town two hours south of Denver. In the Google Maps photo, the sun is shining, the linden tree is leafed out, and the sky is a clear blue. Visible above the slats of the wooden fence is Leo's grapevine, the one descended from the grapes his immigrant parents grew. It is dense and green, smothering its arbor.

Then I see the ghost, and chills run down my spine. He is standing upright inside the mouth of the garage, holding a push broom. A smudge, a blur, a solitary wisp of smoke in Velcro sneakers. He must have stopped sweeping the garage floor to watch the Google photo truck drive by his house. At first, I am pleased to see the ghost of Leo in his garage, his presence tucked into this tiny corner of the internet among his tools and fishing gear, his old Bronco. This is where I'd like to remember him, where he was happy and productive. But later, Beth will tell me that his mind would already have been slipping when this photo was taken in 2012. That was the year he started calling his next-door neighbor, complaining that men were coming out of the television set. For years, Leo had been forgetting things, little things: his order at a restaurant, names and dates. But that all happened after I knew him. Now, when I look at his blurred presence on my computer screen, I see a deterioration, a vanishing act in slow motion.

Beth and I have been talking on the phone for over an hour. She tells me that Dave, her husband, says howdy, but I never hear his voice. I picture him in another room, picking at his guitar or reading the paper. He hasn't seen Krystal in seven years, Beth tells me, not since Leo's funeral. We are a bit like gawkers, Beth and I—slowing to look at the wreckage of the past, teasing it apart, examining it piece by piece. Krystal is the most interesting thing we have in common, maybe the only thing we have in common. We each have our theories, our stories, our scars.

When Beth has a juicy detail to share, she lowers her voice conspiratorially. We are talking about the beginnings now, the period of time when my father and Krystal first met. "You know," Beth says, "when they started dating, Leo told Dave, 'Hey, I think Krystie's a bit of a homewrecker.'"

"Really," I say, unsurprised by the idea that Krystal played a part in the demise of my parents' marriage. I know that my father and Krystal worked together, that my mother had met Krystal at my father's corporate functions before Sam was even born. What surprises me is that Leo knew, that the news had traveled to Cañon City while my brother was still in diapers. Had Krystal told her father that she was seeing a married man with two children? Had he felt guilty on his daughter's behalf?

"Well, by that point she had already been divorced twice," Beth continues. "You know, she got married right out of high school to a guy who had been a football star—she was the cheerleader, that whole deal. They lived in Cañon, and it didn't work out. So, she moves to Denver, gets a job with a golf course design firm, and marries Chad, who's really good-looking, but he's basically a golf course maintenance guy. That lasted awhile. And each time, she's getting closer to the lifestyle she wants—a beautiful house, wealthy friends. But she's always creating these personas, like a shape-shifter. And she's always looking for the person who can get her closer to what she wants."

In my notebook, I scribble *shape-shifter, personas, first husband???*

"I didn't know about her first husband," I say. I am greedy for information. In a 1996 parenting evaluation, the forensic psychologist who observed and interviewed my family noted that Krystal was *once* divorced. A subtle but noticeable detail only because my stepfather had been *twice* divorced, which the psychologist had also noted. Krystal loved to speculate about Cecil's two ex-wives, to cite that aspect of his past as proof that he was unstable, unfit to be a parent. Meanwhile, the skeletons in her closet rattled. *Hypocrite*, I think.

"I don't think she would have wanted you to know," Beth says. "Maybe she thought your dad could get her the life she wanted and was mad at him when he couldn't."

Could it be that we—me, Sam, Dad—were just a stepping stone, a faulty rung in Krystal's climb up the social ladder? What about December 28, her parents' anniversary, the date of Krystal and Dad's wedding? Wasn't that an indication that she wanted this marriage, this family, to work?

But to Krystal, nothing was so important as one's image.

"The thing I don't understand," I tell Beth, "is that she wanted so badly to be our mother, insisted we were a family, called my mom the 'birth mother,' but then she left, without a word to me. I still can't make sense of it. Did she want to be our mom? Or did she just not want our mom to have us?" I trail off, suddenly conscious of what Beth thinks of me, an adult woman who is still tangled in her childhood trauma. Obsessed with the ghosts of her past. Damaged.

"Maybe she was jealous. Jealous of your mom, jealous of you as you got older," Beth says gently, tentatively. "She always liked to be top dog, that's what she wanted."

I pause, taking this explanation in. "I have this random memory," I say, "of one Christmas where Krystal served a really fancy seafood soup with all sorts of mussels and shrimp and fish in it. *Cioppino*, I think she called it. And she was going on and on about how healthy it was, and you just said matter-of-fact, 'You know, shrimp is actually very high in cholesterol.' The whole table went silent, and I thought she was going to *kill* you."

Beth laughs, "I don't remember that, but it doesn't surprise me. It sounds like something I would say. Something interesting to add to the conversation. I wouldn't have meant anything by it."

But you must have meant *something* by it, I want to say, intended or not. You couldn't just contradict Krystal for no reason. Any contrary remark was symbolic, even when that remark was about the cholesterol content of shrimp. One time, Krystal argued with Dad for ten minutes because he told her that no, the days don't keep getting longer throughout summer after the summer solstice. She was convinced that through August, daylight hours would only increase. Finally, Dad simply conceded. It was just easier to let Krystal be right. This is why I remember that Christmas dinner. Beth had taken a stand—albeit a passive-aggressive one—while I slurped fish broth and watched the subtle power dynamics play out. My stepmother's glare could have shattered a crystal goblet, while Beth smoothed her napkin and tucked a strand of hair behind an ear.

Of course, every memory, every flippant remark means something, if only to the people who remember. Otherwise why would this one return to me years later? *Meaning* is what I'm looking for when I peer into the wreckage: salvaged meanings, salvaged memories. Salvage, from the Latin root *salvare*—to save something that is in danger of being destroyed. I think of Leo's ghost, an internet glitch, a moment trapped inside a server. Ephemeral. I am standing there with him, barefoot on the dusty cool of the garage floor, breathing in the scent of linden flowers, of sawdust, oil stains, and old wood. *This means something, right? It has to, doesn't it?* Leo doesn't answer. He doesn't know I'm there.

Soon after we met them, Phyllis and Leo absorbed us into their family, encouraged Sam and me to call them simply "Grandma and Grandpa." We did, though it felt unnatural at first, like playing a role meant for someone else. Looking back, it wasn't as if we had a choice in the matter. I wonder now if they felt pity for their new step-grandchildren, bobbing haplessly among the flotsam and jetsam of their parents' divorce. Were they compensating for what had happened in the past or for what they perceived to be the writing on the wall?

Krystal's parents were an unlikely pairing. Leo was the youngest of five children. His family had immigrated from Italy, and he was the only one born in the US—in Cañon City. He was short and stocky, olive skinned, and wore his salt-and-pepper hair slicked down, neatly parted on the left. My favorite photo of him was taken when he was in the Air Force, a young man of barely twenty with smooth skin and large dark eyes, and the same slicked-down haircut. He had a quick sense of humor and an easy smile that revealed a row of white, perfectly straight, symmetrical teeth—his dentures. I knew that every night he "took his teeth out," just as Phyllis "took her eyes out"—her contacts—and put on thick Coke-bottle glasses that made her face look small and owl-like. I always hoped to see Leo without his teeth in, though I never did.

Phyllis was tall and thin with pale skin and dark, almost black, hair. She was from Sacramento, California, raised by a strict Baptist mother who did not like that Leo was Italian and Catholic. I remember Phyllis watching fiery evangelical church sermons on TV, thumbing through the worn Bible next to her recliner. Whereas Leo seemed unbreakably solid—we called his hands catcher's mitts because his callused fingers were thick as sausages—Phyllis was bony and delicate. My father liked to joke that at dinner she would heap spaghetti or lasagna on everyone's plates, then say, "Oh, and I'll just have this little piece of lettuce."

Phyllis sewed quilts and clothes and was a self-taught oil painter, skills which she attempted to pass on to me, but did not stick. We did one oil painting together. Phyllis sketched the design: a simple, bucolic landscape. There was a pond bordered by cattails and feathery trees, and a sky filled with large puffy clouds. We set up the easel and canvas on the back porch. The long paintbrush wobbled in my small hand, but Phyllis gripped my fingers, moving my hand with hers. The firmness of her hold surprised me.

"Here. I'm going to help you," she said. "We don't want to waste any paint. This is good paint."

I can do it myself, I wanted to say. *Just show me how, and I can do it!* When I did crafts with my mother, she let me make what I wanted, not worrying about the final product. But Phyllis held my hand tightly in hers. I started to wriggle free, but something stopped me. I loved my new grandparents—my new stepfamily—but I also understood that I was the interloper in their lives, pretending to belong, adopting the customs, when really, I was different. I sensed that deep down their love might be conditional, and that my best behavior was required. I let my hand submit to hers.

Krystal mounted the painting in an ornate gold frame and hung it on the wall in my bedroom at their house. As the years went by, I absorbed and memorized each brushstroke, so that as I got older, I came to feel trapped beside that stagnant pond, imprisoned inside that gold frame. Later, after Krystal left, I stuffed the painting in a black trash bag along with all the other things I was throwing away. The painting was a fragment of a past life that I could no longer return to, that I no longer *wanted* to return to. The painting belonged to the little girl who played her role so convincingly that she almost forgot who she was. I couldn't bear to look at her.

Leo had friends and relatives all over Cañon, and he would take us with him to go visiting. I came to know the city through its retirees, many of whom were first- or second-generation immigrants. Leo had worked his entire career as an electrician at the cement manufacturer outside Cañon, perhaps making cement that was used to construct the walls and foundation of the federal prison. Most of his friends were his old coworkers, and he spoke of them as though they were delegates from Ellis Island, amiably calling them "polacks" and "krauts" and "wops." "Hey Carlo, you dumb wop!" he might say warmly to his oldest and best Italian friend. "Hey, Leonardo!" Carlo would respond in accented English, and they'd laugh and slap each other on the back.

Leo was proudly Italian—or as he sometimes pronounced it, *EYE-tal-ian*—though he'd forgotten most of the language of his youth. He reminisced about his father harvesting grapes and making wine, about his mother rolling out pasta dough on the kitchen table with a broomstick.

"Have you heard the joke about the Italian tires?" Leo liked to say. "Dago here and dago there, and when dago flat, dago wop wop wop." I would laugh, though I wasn't exactly sure what was funny. Now I wonder if Leo's self-deprecation was a form of self-protection, a coat of armor that had formed during the years when he had been called a "dumb wop," not as a joke but as an insult.

In 2015, *Atlas Obscura* ran a story on a "mystifying" photo of forty robed and hooded Klansmen posed on a Ferris wheel in Cañon City. The photo was taken at a traveling amusement park in 1926, four years before Leo was born, and the contrast between the whimsical carnival ride and the grim, faceless presence of the KKK is chilling. At that time, the unusual sight would have been the Ferris wheel—a novelty then—not the hooded figures. Through the 1920s, the Klan controlled all levels of Colorado's state government, and their central hub was Cañon City. In the mining-turned-prison town, the KKK focused their ire on the new wave of immigrants from Southern Europe who were mostly Catholic and believed to be stealing jobs and disrupting the town's temperate culture. Leo's family would have arrived in Cañon during this period. Had they been harassed, bullied, terrorized? Perhaps this legacy is why there is no synagogue in Cañon, and why the city is nearly ninety-five percent white.

"Unfortunately, the household that Krystal grew up in was focused on appearances, for the girls especially," Beth says. "You had to be pretty, have your hair nice, behave a certain way. Your value was placed on the way you looked. And I'm not a psychiatrist, but it seems to me like

Krystal put all her self-worth in her appearance. It fed into her need for approval and adulation."

I remember the childhood photos of Krystal, displayed in Leo and Phyllis's home. In an early school photo, she is wearing a pale blue sweater and a little gold cross necklace. Her blonde hair is curled and stiff, the line of her bangs so straight it must have been cut with a ruler. She looks more like a doll than a child. I picture Phyllis, the wisp of her waist, the sharp blades of her shoulder bones, her coiffed black hair and pink lipstick. In the rafters of Leo and Phyllis's garage, stored in mint condition, were the vintage Barbies that once belonged to Krystal and her sister. The Barbies wore tiny hand-sewn bell bottoms and mini mod dresses. They had slender torsos and pointed toes, shiny blonde hair.

"Was Phyllis the one who was focused on appearances?" I ask, already knowing the answer. I recalled her firm grip on my hand as I held the paintbrush.

"Well, it sure wasn't Leo," Beth says.

Phyllis died of complications from a stroke shortly before Christmas, 2001. I was twelve. Her body was so emaciated that the doctors in the hospital asked when she had stopped eating. Our jokes about how Phyllis ate like a bird now seemed like grim premonitions. Her funeral was held inside the Baptist church she belonged to in Cañon City. Though I had been to mass with Leo countless times, I had never been inside Phyllis's church before. It was a plain building with a low, peaked roof. No crucifix hung behind the altar. No stained glass windows. Had Phyllis come here while we were at St. Michael's? How much did I really know about the woman who kept Werther's butterscotch candies and balled-up tissues in her purse? I had always viewed her with a mixture of love and fear. Now I realized she could have been a stranger.

And she was a stranger, to the extent that any adult is a stranger to a child. Many years later, my father would tell me that Phyllis had once had an affair with a man who attended her church. While Leo was at work and the kids were at school, Phyllis would covertly meet up across town with her Evangelical lover. One of Leo's brothers noticed her odd behavior, eventually put two and two together, then alerted Leo to her infidelity. But unlike my mother's parents who divorced when my mother was a teenager, Krystal's parents stayed married. They were religious. They lived in a small town. Apparently, it was all water under the bridge. "Did you notice that Leo never spoke of Phyllis again after she died?" my father asked me. I had not. I assumed that Leo had been grief-stricken. I hadn't accounted for other possibilities. What else had I not noticed? What other secrets were lurking in plain sight?

Leo and Phyllis had always seemed to me like the kind of old-timey grandparents who existed on TV: *Leave It to Beaver* churchgoing people, living inside a bubble of small-town innocence. I felt that theirs was the sort of life I was supposed to want, and I embraced it wholeheartedly. I loved the unfinished "utility room" that Leo had wired so that the light turned on automatically when you opened the door. I loved the house's many contraptions: Phyllis's bread machine that produced steaming cubes of fresh bread, the swamp cooler in the living room window, the electric trash compactor, the pop can crusher. I loved the garage, which housed the scooters and bikes Sam and I played on, and where Leo had hung the signs: *Parking for Italians Only* and *Trespassers Will Be Shot, Survivors Will Be Shot Again*. I even loved the cold, earthy smell of the garage refrigerator which was used only to store soda pop and Styrofoam containers of live nightcrawlers. I had surrendered myself to their sensory world. I had painted myself into a make-believe life, a make-believe family.

The Cañon City I knew doesn't exist anymore; perhaps it never did. Cañon was not and is not innocent. Its shame is buried beneath the surface, its guilt displaced and hidden from view. Beyond the city limits, twenty percent of the county population sits locked behind bars. Sometimes we can't see what's hiding in front of us. What I want to know, and which neither Beth nor I could possibly understand, is how much my step-grandparents had known about their daughter. How much were they responsible for the person Krystal had become?

It's hard for me to hear Beth talk about Leo's last years. She tells me that Alzheimer's turned him violent and fearful, that Dave had to move him to a facility where the patients lived in rooms with white walls and the toilet seats painted fire engine red. But before his memory had completely gone, Leo and Dave had made all the end-of-life arrangements. Leo had even picked out the music he wanted at his funeral: Dean Martin. I remembered belting out the words to "Volare" and "You're Nobody 'Til Somebody Loves You" in the kitchen as he stirred a pot of tomato sauce. There was no artist he loved more than Dean Martin.

Beth tells me that the funeral was at St. Michael's Church. Krystal arrived wearing a tight black skirt with a long slit up each side, a new boob job on display. She was accompanied by an SUV full of Spanish-speaking workers from her landscaping business. According to Beth, each of the workers had a red rose, and when the funeral ended, they walked down the center aisle, taking turns laying the roses on Leo's casket. Krystal always loved the theatricality of a grand gesture. "Family is everything" was my stepmother's motto, but here, she had chosen to surround herself with her hired hands so that she could be the blonde bombshell in the spotlight—adored, beloved. Is this what Sam and Dad and I had been for her? A built-in set of admirers? We may have looked like we played for the same team, but it was a trick of the eye. In the end, the team captain jumped ship.

I was eighteen the last time I saw Leo. I had no way of knowing that he would soon begin a rapid descent into memory loss and illness. Or that my father and stepmother's marriage was ready to implode. While I was away at college, Krystal left without saying goodbye, without offering me explanations or apologies. She was there, and then she was not. I knew from my dad that she had been seeing another man, someone who worked on her landscaping crew. I knew that she never wanted to see me or my brother or my father ever again.

The end of their marriage was like a death, in that a portion of my life, my family, my identity had been taken away, pruned like a rotted tree limb. I was angry and confused. I was grieving what had never existed. I felt the way I had when Phyllis died—as if the truth were behind a locked door, the key thrown away. The difference this time was that everyone was still alive. Even now, memories of my stepfamily return with the pain of a phantom limb. I still struggle with the question of how to mourn the loss of a family who was never mine to begin with.

A year after the divorce, I wrote Leo an email. I told him I missed him, and said I was sorry I hadn't written sooner—I was still trying to work through my complicated emotions. He responded the next day.

> Hi Poopsie, you will never believe how happy I was to hear from you, and I had to wipe a couple of tears clean. It was hard for me to handle the divorce but I'm hanging in there. I always say that if you don't have a family you don't have anything. Lots of hugs and kisses to you, CIAO, GRANDPA.

We emailed a couple more times that year, but after that, I never reached out or heard from him again.

A memory comes to mind, of the time Phyllis accidentally slammed Leo's finger in the door of their Crown Victoria. I was there, standing on the front lawn, watching. I remember the thud of the car door, and how Leo grunted in pain, how he grimaced and shook his hand, his blood spattering on the snow. How he said, "I'm okay, I'm okay," and went inside and wrapped his finger in a cloth napkin until the blood seeped through, and then took that napkin off, and replaced it with another napkin, on and on until the bleeding stopped.

The pain would have been excruciating. We hovered, feeling our own phantom hurts while Leo nursed his hand, staunched the bleeding, smothered the pain. "It's nothing," he said. "Just a little cut." He never went to the doctor, and his meaty pointer finger healed crooked, the top joint permanently bent, as if his finger was taking a perpetual bow. "I can point around the corner now," he joked.

We've all healed in grotesque ways, denied our pain. We keep moving ahead, and yet always we are peering over our shoulders, looking back toward the past.

Dave and Beth have been packing up their belongings. They have a week left before they officially retire, and then they are moving from Texas to a mountain town in Colorado. They bought land there years ago and built a house with a balcony that looks out onto the surrounding peaks. They'll only be an hour from Cañon City, though there wouldn't be much reason for them to visit. Leo's house sold quickly after he moved to the nursing home.

"I've never driven this far by myself before," Beth says. "Dave will have the dogs in his car. I'll have the cats. They'll be on anti-anxiety meds, of course. But I'm still nervous."

"You'll be great," I say. "It will be a nice, scenic drive."

"And listen, once we get settled in, you'll have to come for a visit. We'd love to have you. Serious."

I picture myself on Dave and Beth's balcony, an iced tea in hand, the smell of juniper and pinion pine, the warm Colorado sun on my face. Wouldn't it be nice, I think, to see them on my own terms, to rebuild a relationship whose foundation was rotten to the core? But what is left to rebuild? All Beth and I have are the ghosts and secrets of the past. There's nothing left to salvage.

"I will," I say. "I definitely will."

The Burning House

I've only walked out of two movies in my life—once with my mom and once with my dad. The first was *What's Eating Gilbert Grape*. It came out when I was four, which meant Sam was only a year old, and Mom had inexplicably taken us to the theater to see it. My memories of that day are hazy. Of the movie, all I remember is a very fat woman in a recliner. And then I remember Mom ushering us out of the darkened theater. That was the year that Dad left.

After a relationship ends, everything takes on weighted significance; the subtlest of plot points drip with accusation. Movies are designed to make us feel something, to needle their way below our skin. A good movie can be too much for someone whose heart is an open wound. Why had we gone to see *that* movie, about a single mother whose disabilities prevent her from properly caring for her children? What had Mom seen or felt that made her need to leave? Or had Sam simply been crying?

Fifteen years later, in the wake of another failing marriage, Dad and I walked out of *Synecdoche, New York*, which we went to see a week or maybe a month after what I have come to think of as The Day When Everything Changed. For whatever reason, I didn't write about the movie—or what I saw of it—in my journal, though I journaled meticulously that year. Maybe it didn't seem important enough, or maybe I wanted to forget it. Maybe I knew I *wouldn't* forget it. I didn't even keep the ticket stub in the back pocket of that worn black Moleskine notebook, where I liked to store other little notes, tickets, photos. I didn't want evidence.

Synecdoche follows Caden, played by Philip Seymour Hoffman, a middle-aged playwright who wants to create a play that encompasses the meaning—or meaninglessness—of life, even as a mysterious, fatal disease slowly ravages his body.

I picked the movie because it seemed artsy and intellectual, which is how I liked to think of myself now that I knew the difference between modernism and postmodernism, between absurdism and existentialism. And Dad agreed because he liked Philip Seymour Hoffman. Movies are what we did in those days, during my weekend visits home from college. They were a distraction from what was really going on in our lives. But that particular movie cut too close to the truth for us. A woman buys a burning house, knowing that the fire will eventually kill her. A tattoo turns poisonous. A painter becomes more famous the tinier her paintings get; her patrons have to use magnifying glasses to see them. The life Dad had built with Krystal was shrinking into nothingness. The house they had bought was burning, and still Dad was sure he could salvage it on his own. Meanwhile I was just trying to salvage Dad.

"I can't take this, let's get out of here," Dad said at some point, and we made our way out of the theater with relief. And where did we go next? I have a memory of being in Dad's old "Beamer," as he called it, at night on Arapahoe Road, the blur of headlights cutting through the dark. There was the weight of silence, of words that could not be unsaid, mistakes that could not be undone. But that memory could have been from any night that year.

As usual, here I am, trying to make meaning out of the scraps.

A week or a month earlier

On the day when everything changes, I am eating noodles with my father at a new Asian fusion restaurant in our suburb. The restaurant is very on-trend, with warm wood undertones and funky metal accents; a sleek digital menu hangs above the counter where we place our orders. Since I left for college the year before, it seems that every time I come back home some trendy new restaurant or Pilates gym has sprouted up. The suburb grows larger like a living organism, devouring the open prairie. Eventually nothing wild will be left.

Being away has given me fresh eyes with which to hate this place. A *suburban wasteland*, I've labeled it in my journal. My hatred is self-protective; it makes me feel superior and apart. I won't understand until much later how much this suburb shaped me, how much it is a part of me. I came of age among its gently curving asphalt roads, its cul-de-sacs, its tones of beige.

Dad and I sit across the table from each other. I am facing the window, and he is facing the back of the restaurant. I study his face, his mustache now flecked with gray. The wisps of hair on his head and above his ears are neatly brushed. I picture his brush, its soft black bristles and solid wooden handle. I always found it funny that my balding father owned the nicest hairbrush I'd ever seen. Until recently, I have always thought of my father as a successful, powerful person. He is the kind of man who gets his work shirts dry cleaned with extra starch, speaks and writes with an enormous vocabulary, has an encyclopedic knowledge of geography, history, science. As a child I always tried to emulate him, sought his approval, wanted to make him proud. For example, when he began working as a financial planner at a large investment management company, I told everyone that I, too, wanted to be a financial planner when I grew up. I, too, wanted to work in a skyscraper, in an office with big glass windows doing—I'm not sure what he actually did. The only time I visited was for "Take Your Daughter to Work Day," but I didn't see any work being done. The secretary took me and the other little girls to the board room to paint our nails.

That was many years ago, back when he and Krystal were still newlyweds, still very much in love, as it seemed to me and everyone around them. The man across the table from me now is sadder, smaller in his worn brown leather jacket. It's been nearly a year since Sam started living full-time at Mom's, since Krystal bagged up everything that he left behind and threw it out with the trash, including his books, clothes, photos, and the model airplanes and pinewood derby cars that he and Dad had built together. Dad had watched as Krystal—twenty pounds slimmer and seven shades tanner than she had been when they married—disposed of his son's belongings. He is now estranged from his teenage son who lives five blocks away. And where is Krystal, anyways?

"I feel like I don't fit in," I tell Dad, poking my chopsticks absentmindedly into the bowl of udon noodles in front of me. "Everyone at school is so immature and obsessed with their appearances and drinking and going to parties. No one is *real*." I don't tell him about my long walks past the college sub shops and the grungy bars that sell cheap pitchers of Long Island iced tea, past Fraternity Row on The Hill, through the nice, old neighborhood where the professors live, and to the historic cemetery. How I sit there beneath a tree, writing melodramatic, soul-searching paragraphs in my journal. How I think about mortality and think about myself thinking about mortality. How everything feels monumental and tragic.

"And how are your grades? Still working hard?" Dad asks. I wonder if he's even heard me.

"They're good. My research internship is going well, and my adviser said I have enough credits to add a third major if I wanted to."

"Good job, kiddo. I'm so proud of you." Tears well in his eyes. In my journal, I will later describe him as "dewy-eyed," which is a term Dad himself uses to describe the welling of tears, the way regret, or sadness, or love, or a mixture of all three can crest over him like a powerful wave.

Something is wrong, but I'm not sure what it is.

Two weeks before this day, the day when everything changed, Sam visited me at my university. I was surprised by how tall he was, at his newly sprouted facial hair. He was sixteen, going on seventeen, and now driving Cecil's old Toyota Corolla that we had named Hank. He came up to Boulder on a Friday, and we walked around the campus. We didn't talk about Dad's drinking, or how Krystal had called the cops on Sam when he spit on the ground as she drove by. We talked about college.

I pointed out the buildings where I took my English and political science classes, gave him a tour of the stacks at the library ("Don't be one of those students who never checks out a book," I said sternly), then we ate falafel sandwiches on Pearl Street. He drank in the sights and sounds of college life, and I could see his mind churning with the possibilities of being "away." I pretended that it was all as good as it seemed. I was his big sister, and being apart from him had softened our relationship. We said things now like "I miss you." He burned me mix CDs filled with his new favorite indie bands and singer-songwriters. I wanted him to be happy, and I wanted to protect him in the ways I had failed to protect him from Dad and Krystal in the years before.

Sam sat in on a macroeconomics lecture because he wanted to major in business one day, and then I took him to my Portuguese class. I knew he wanted to make a lot of money, be successful. This drive to make money scared me. I worried that like Dad, Sam would fly too close to the sun and scorch his wings. Money and success in itself seemed an empty goal. But if I was being honest with myself, my goal felt empty, too. I didn't care about money; I was driven by the need to one day get as far away as I could from here. (From my journal: *If I stay here I'll die. But if I'm not happy here, will I be happy somewhere else?*)

That night I drove back home with Sam, slept in my old bedroom at Mom's, did my laundry. Saturday, I went to Dad's. Something was *off* about the yellow house where I had spent half my childhood. Maybe it was that Sam no longer lived there. Or that Krystal's heavy antiques were dustier than usual. Stacks of old newspapers sat in the corner by the kitchen table. The refrigerator was empty save for a few single-serving containers of low-fat, sugar-free yogurt. The house itself felt lonely, neglected. With forced cheer, Dad told me we were having company that night—his old friend Bill from grad school and Bill's daughter McKenzie. Krystal was always the one who prepared for company, who lit scented candles, put *Piano by the Sea* on the CD player, made fancy appetizers, mixed cosmopolitan martinis in an iced shaker. She was nowhere to be found.

"Where's Krystie?" I asked. It had been months since I had seen my stepmother, spoken to her. And honestly, I did not want to see her or speak to her, but her absence was conspicuous. She must have known I was coming. Was she avoiding me? This was not a new feeling. A year earlier, during the fall of my freshman year of college, I had written in my journal: *Krystie has been really weird lately. Every time I talk on the phone with her I feel like she hates me. It's so weird. Ever since...well before I left she was acting pissed.*

"Working," he said.

We went to the Walmart Supercenter on Arapaho Road, where Dad bought four ribeye steaks. They were bloody and outrageously expensive and each larger than my head. Then we went to the liquor store where he bought margarita mix, tequila, wine. I can't remember if we got any vegetables. (In my journal I mention steak, and I mention tequila. *Over one hundred dollars worth of food and drinks for a single meal.*) Regardless, the gesture felt tragic in its extravagance. We got home, and Krystal was still not there. Dad did not seem surprised. I pretended not to be either.

It was cold and dark outside, and we had trouble seeing the gas grill. I brought out a flashlight, and Dad found the dial on the propane, cursing under his breath. Finally, flames burst forth. He unwrapped the expensive steaks from their dripping packages and slapped them on the grill. Neither of us was sure how long they would take to cook.

I guessed thirty minutes, and Dad guessed fifteen. It didn't occur to me then to call Cecil who often grilled flank steaks and hamburgers. He would have known how long to cook the meat, how to check the internal temperature, monitor the flame. In those days, I still worked hard to compartmentalize my life with each household, to keep my parents as far from each other as was possible. Old habits die hard.

"Do we season them?" I asked.

"Sure, why not," Dad said with a shrug, a blank look on his face. As a child, I had always looked to him for answers—he was a man who read calculus books for fun, who liked to give impromptu lessons on roadside geologic formations. Now without Krystal, he seemed rudderless, unsure of the most basic of tasks. As if on cue, we both began to laugh—at our own helplessness, at the absurdity of the giant steaks. I was afraid that if I stopped laughing, I would cry.

Inside, Dad poured the margarita mix into the blender with ice and tequila. I didn't ask why he was making margaritas in November. I was still caught up in the spirit of reckless abandon. And something else: defiance. This was our *unbirthday* party—we were doing things the opposite of how my stepmother, an immaculate entertainer and Martha Stewart devotee, would want them done. She would not approve, and that felt good.

Around seven, Dad's friend Bill arrived with his daughter McKenzie, who was still in high school. Their arrival reminded us to check on the steaks, which had burned to a crisp on the grill. The evening was awkward, the amount of alcohol oddly inappropriate. Dad talked non-stop. I barely talked at all. Krystal never called.

Later that night, I was almost asleep in my old bedroom, in my old bed, when I heard the garage door open, then heard her footfalls on the stairs. In the morning, she was gone before I woke up. It was the last time we'd ever be under the same roof.

In my dream, I am sitting at a long table, surrounded by friends and family.

I know them but I can't make out their faces. My vision is blurred, as if looking through a Vaseline-smudged window, my body sluggish as if weighted down by sand. Even so, I can tell the faces are watching me. My stepmother is the only one speaking, and everyone is listening to her. She is listing off my sins, and for each one, she places a rosary around my hands, which are clasped in front of me as if in prayer. I am crying so hard that I can't speak, can't say that these sins don't belong to me, that she has it all wrong. The rosaries, though, are beautiful, made of polished stones. They are heavy and my arms ache with their weight. And then I realize that the reason my friends and family are seated around me at the long table is because we are at a Passover Seder. And Krystal has prepared the meal. I wake up in a cold sweat.

In the restaurant with my dewy-eyed dad on the day when everything changes, I am still trying to pinpoint what exactly is wrong. (From my journal: *Things change so—suddenly. Or maybe they change gradually, but we just don't realize what has happened until the moment hits us.*)

Dad has an untouched bowl of pad Thai in front of him. On his left hand, he wears his wedding ring. A simple gold band. On his right hand, he wears a large silver ring embedded with a polished chunk of *lapis lazuli*, a memento from his time in Chihuahua, Mexico, earlier this year. He was working on a project at a gold mine in the remote high desert without cell service for over a month. He came back with the ring and hundreds of photos of the mine and of the big trucks, their tires the size of mobile homes. (And what was Krystal doing while he was gone? Who was keeping her company? *Her phone was still on, but she didn't answer my calls.*)

"How's Krystie been?" I ask. This seems to be, perhaps, a safer question than asking *Where has Krystie been?* I am doing my best to stay neutral, though my feelings toward her have hardened in the last months. (*I love my memories (the good ones) with [Krystal]*, I had written in my journal. *But I can't bring myself to love her now. She is anti-Semitic, racist, arrogant, vain. Their home is not my home.*)

"Her landscaping business is booming," Dad says, as if reading from a script. "She's landed some big clients. Her clients absolutely worship her." He pauses. "And she's thinking of buying a plane ticket to Wisconsin to see Kevin run in his cross country meet next week."

Not that I really *want* to see her, but this last part irks me. No, I am more than irked. I am irate. "So, she can fly across the country to see her nephew, but she can't drive forty-five minutes to Boulder to see her stepdaughter? She can't pick up her phone when it rings?"

Dad is silent for a moment, as if deciding whether or not he wants to tell the truth, to cross the point of no return. He sighs deeply. He is plunging in and taking me with him, a hostage. Later, I will wonder if I had ever known the truth before this moment, if everything before was just a performance, a facade. Becoming an adult means peeling back the lies of childhood, one after the other, like sloughing off layers of dead skin.

"She has this switch," Dad says. "And once you flip it off, you can't flip it back on." I sit so still that I might not be breathing. "And I don't know why, but she can't stand you. She thinks you're a spy for your mom, that you only want to see me when you want money, that all you want is to get laid, and that you have risqué stuff on your Facebook."

What the fuck? I am ready to explode. "None of that stuff is true. A spy for my mom? Risqué stuff on my Facebook? What does that even mean? I barely even post photos of my friends. That's insane. That's..." My chest constricts; my whole body feels cold. *Risqué.* Krystal wouldn't have used the term "risqué." She would have said *slutty, skanky, little whore.* I can almost see her sneer, feel the rough jab of her finger in my sternum, the spray of her spittle on my face.

"I don't know what you've done to her, Lauren Lou. You've never done anything wrong," Dad says.

"I know," I reply, and I resent my years of good behavior, my obedience. My paper napkin is nearly in shreds in my lap. Around us, people are eating their noodles—some with wooden chopsticks, some with forks. A group of high schoolers sits in a booth in the corner. A family walks past us, the father holding the table number and a tray full of fizzy drinks, the mother scouting an open spot. At our little table, time has stopped. The world flows past us and we stand still, like a boulder in a stream.

"I was actually glad when Sam went to live with his mom because no one should have to put up with that as a kid. She was calling him a 'worthless piece of shit.' My parents didn't treat me like that. Her parents didn't treat her like that. I was just afraid she was going to start slapping him around. And now, Lauren, I think I'm on the outside, too."

Dad wipes his eyes, and only then do I realize that I'm crying, too. I hope the people at the tables around us aren't watching this sad spectacle. I feel like I've opened the wrong dressing room door and accidentally glimpsed a naked stranger inside.

"She's saved up about fifty to sixty thousand in a private savings account and I think she's waiting until the end of the year, and then she's going to blow out of town," Dad says, calmly now, as if he's a witness giving testimony under oath. He tells me that he's installed a GPS tracking device on Krystal's car, that he thinks she's having an affair with a man named Alejandro because she doesn't come home at night and claims she is sleeping in her car (but who knows where she's really sleeping), that she is obsessed with the Mexican workers she's hired for her landscaping company and talks incessantly about how much they adore her, that she thinks she is invincible, that she wants to get a boob job, that she's stopped answering his calls, that she told Leo that she wished she'd never met anyone with the last name Rhoades because we've screwed up her life.

Two weeks later, I sat in the stacks of the library, despairing over an essay I was writing for my British and Irish Novels class about Samuel Beckett's *Molloy*. In the first half of the novel, there are two paragraphs. The second paragraph lasts eighty pages. I didn't enjoy the book. I became lost and confused in the ramblings of what seemed to be a semi-incoherent mind. But I diligently plodded through because—well, because it felt important. My inner world might have been crumbling, but I was nothing if not an exemplary student.

Molloy, my professor had told us, was an *absurdist* novel. Dr. White was a large man, with dandruff flakes on his dark corduroy blazers. On the blackboard he had drawn a Venn diagram. On one side he wrote "Absurdism," on the other "Existentialism."

"Both posit that the universe is inherently meaningless," he had said. "An existentialist would say that we must create our own meaning. Beckett, on the other hand, is more interested in the tension that comes from trying to make meaning in a meaningless world."

I thought about the steak and tequila. I thought about my stepmother wanting a boob job. I thought about the secrets Dad had shared with me and the hours that followed and how they weighed on me like the stones that Molloy put in his pockets, put in his mouth. I thought about how I had entered college as a good Catholic girl, a recent convert, and how over the course of the last year, my faith in God (and especially a Christian God) had withered into a dead thing. (From my journal: *I miss that faith in something . . . it was a decrepit sort of faith at best, although I did a good job of deceiving myself otherwise.*) I thought about how I could not stop eating, could not stop thinking about eating. *Trying to make meaning in a meaningless world.* That's exactly what it felt like I was doing.

The titular character Molloy laments: "My life, my life now I speak of it as something over, now as of a joke which still goes on, and it is neither, for at the same time it is over and it goes on, and is there any tense for that?"

Molloy's life is irrelevant, I wrote in my essay, because *his actions achieve nothing—he never reaches the punch line of the joke. Events occur, but they hold no meaning. His life consists of a string of signifiers with no attached signifieds.*

Was I Molloy, and was he I? In my journal, I wrote that I was, *A writer who doesn't write, a believer who doesn't believe.* I despaired over my eating habits, how at night, alone in my dorm room I mechanically ate Oreos and Nature Valley granola bars until my stomach felt bloated and tight. On these nights when I lost control, I biked to the rec center and punished myself by sweating for an hour on the elliptical then doing twenty minutes of push-ups and core work—or, if the rec center had already closed, I would sprint up the outdoor stairs at the planetarium, avoiding patches of ice. I came back to my dorm room drenched in sweat and then passed out on my bed. The next day I would drink only water and chew through handfuls of sugarless gum. When I felt like I was starving, I binged, and the whole cycle started over again. I couldn't escape. This joke went on and on.

Meanwhile, Dad was slowly deflating. In the last week, he had been laid off. He was losing weight, waking up early to go on runs—something that he hadn't done in years, but which I believed was related to stress and his inability to sleep. He told me he was saying the rosary every night, that he was trying to clean up after himself, to stop cussing, to only drink when Krystal was there.

When I had gone to mass with Dad the weekend before, pretending to be a good Catholic, a man and woman came in late, slid into our pew. The woman handed Dad his sunglasses so she wouldn't sit on them. For an instant I thought she was Krystal and that the man with her was Alejandro, though I had no idea what Alejandro looked like. A sense of panic stayed with me for the rest of mass. (*Does Krystal even exist?* I wrote. *Is she hollow, made of straw? Am I?*)

Molloy says: "Yes, there were times when I forgot not only who I was but that I was, forgot to be." In my essay, I wrote that for Molloy, *the body itself is a grotesque form of torture. The body delineates the limits of the self; paradoxically, its decay fortifies an awareness of selfhood.* Dad had forgotten who he was without his second wife. He was consumed by his need to get her back, and I was consumed by a loss that I couldn't define. This psychic loss manifested itself in my body, in my insatiable hunger, my desperation to control what I could not.

How long do we stay at the noodle restaurant? Long enough for Dad to tell me everything he has bottled up for years—the lies, the deceit, the false accusations. The GPS tracker he secretly installed on my stepmother's Dodge Durango, the car she uses for work, hauling plants and mulch and garden tools. I picture the tracker like a beetle, hiding under the hood. I hate Krystal, but the tracking beetle scares me. I'm only nineteen, still boyfriend-less, still a virgin, but even I know there are some things you shouldn't tell your own child, things you shouldn't do to the partner you claim to love.

When we exit into the parking lot, the sun has disappeared behind the mountains and the sky glows a fiery orange. Cars whiz by, carrying people on their way to dinner at Outback Steakhouse, or to pick up shampoo at the Super Target, or to see a movie at the AMC theater. Dad's car is a gold 1995 BMW—not even vintage now in 2008—that Krystal insisted he have (she bought herself a black one). It has been plagued with mechanical issues ever since they brought it home. I slide into the tan leather passenger seat, inhale the old car smell. This car is symbolic of their marriage: a vanity purchase, an empty promise, a money pit. The karmic car.

Dad turns the key in the ignition, pumps the gas pedal, and the engine sputters and finally roars to life. We are going to the new James Bond movie, the twenty-second in the series, called *Quantum of Solace*. How much is a "quantum of solace"? How do you even measure comfort or consolation? Nothing makes sense in this new version of reality, but we need a distraction. Anything to keep us from going back to the house and its quiet accusation.

I only loosely pay attention to the screen, distracted by thoughts of Krystal and her lover. Daniel Craig shoots everyone in sight, his mouth a grim line. A wall of mirrors shatters in a fiery explosion.

Next to me, Dad fidgets in his seat. He checks his phone frequently, flipping it open to reveal a glowing square, then snapping it shut again, apparently not finding what he's looking for. He leans forward in his seat, eyes shifting from the screen to the exit sign.

"Dad, are you okay?" I whisper.

"Yeah, yeah, yeah," he shakes his head and waves me off. Leans back.

Neither of us wanted snacks or soda. Neither of us is hungry. We are watching a James Bond movie dry-mouthed and empty-handed, gritting our teeth until the end. I have never realized how lonely James Bond must be. How solitary and tragic a figure he is, carrying a load of trauma and guilt around with him. Or maybe he is a psychopath. In the first half of the film he kills at least four dozen people. Without even a quantum of remorse.

Really, the movie is beside the point. The credits roll. The lights come on. Dad leaps from his seat. "Let's go, kiddo." He is pushing past people to get out of the theater. He cups his hand behind him while he walks, a signal that he wants me to grab it like when I was a little kid, and I do. He pulls me forward, and then we are out of the theater, jogging through the parking lot. I zip my coat against the chill November air.

"Why are we running? What's the rush?" I've never seen Dad like this, panicked, like someone is chasing him.

"It's Krystal. I have a bad feeling. I just know she's up to something." The engine sputters again. What if we're stranded here? Would we have to call Krystal to come pick us up? Would she even come?

"Dad."

"I need to get on the computer, check the GPS. Find out where she's headed."

Miraculously, the car starts again. We zoom out of the parking lot. Dad's eyes are laser focused on the road, his hands gripped tightly on the leather-covered steering wheel, a suburban James Bond. The gold Beamer speeds down Arapahoe Road, gunning through yellow lights.

A right on Havana Road. A careening right on Maplewood Drive. A left on Iola Way. The streets are quiet, the neighbors' porch lights illuminated like tiny beacons. What fresh discovery awaits us at the old Dell computer in the upstairs guest bedroom? Probably nothing. Probably nothing. *Probably nothing.*

"It's probably nothing, Dad. I don't think you need to check it," I say. He switches on the lights in the dark house, already halfway up the stairs, not even bothering to take off his shoes. Krystal would scold him if she were here. The computer chimes on, the modem fans whir.

This is the same computer where, years ago, Krystal discovered my MySpace page. Sat me down in the rolling chair where Dad sits now and pointed to photos of my friends and me at the bowling alley wearing shorts and tank tops as if they were evidence she had collected, pointed to a MySpace high school group I was part of, then clicked on the group's members, revealing a list of mostly strangers, including someone whose screenname was *clit_commander*. I didn't know who this person was, had never seen the screen name before. How long had she been lurking, digging, just to find them? Their profile photo was an image of a cartoon gorilla, faintly sinister.

"You're a slut, Lauren. A slut." I was fourteen, and despite having watched videos about STIs and rolled a condom over a banana in freshman health class, I still had no idea what a clit was, or how this stranger's unsavory identity reflected on me. I deleted my MySpace profile that night.

Dad types something into the internet browser. A portal comes up. He types in a username and then a password, pecking the keys with his index fingers. A wheel spins, and then a map spreads across the screen.

In 2001, when Google Earth was unveiled, Dad brought Sam and me upstairs to this computer. Together, we traveled to the Egyptian pyramids, saw our houses from above, flew to the Grand Canyon, to Paris, to Mumbai, across the Midwest's patchwork farmland. We were filled with awe at how different the world looked from up high, how small it all seemed. Now, we are zoomed in on a grid of streets in a part of town unfamiliar to me.

"Oh no, she's headed out to Aurora," Dad groans, his face edging closer to the screen, eyes squinted. The computer bathes us in its blue light, and I am reminded of the fish tank I used to have in my bedroom at Mom's house. I see it then, the red dot that must be his wife. The lone, blinking red dot traveling down the arteries of the map in a direction that means nothing to me. *Let her go*, I want to say.

"She's headed to Aurora," Dad repeats. "She's with that Mexican guy. She's going to a hotel. Oh god. I'm going out there."

"You don't know that, Dad. Please, please don't go. This is a bad idea." My voice is shrill, but Dad isn't listening. He scribbles something down on a piece of paper. Street names, an address. He has always had an impeccable sense of direction, a love of maps.

"Lauren Lou, I need you to do me a favor," he says. He sounds exhausted.

"No, I don't want anything to do with this. This is a terrible idea."

"I just need you to watch this GPS here. I'll call you, and you update me on where the little red dot is going, okay? Easy."

I am crying again. Maybe he won't go because he'll see that what he is doing is causing me distress. Maybe he will choose me this time. "I'm not going to do that, Dad. I have a bad feeling about this. What if something happens?"

But the tears don't work. Dad zips up his leather jacket. Stuffs the folded paper with the address in his pocket. I am afraid he is going to hurt someone, afraid he is going to wreck the gold Beamer, afraid he will harm himself.

"I need you to do this for me, Lauren. Please." What if *I* am the linchpin, the one who allows everything to go wrong?

"Please, Lauren. Please, please, please." He is one step away from getting down on his knees to beg. This is the man who used to call himself "the 800-pound gorilla."

"Fine," I say.

I watch the door close behind him. The puff of cold night air sends a chill down my spine. I am alone in the house. The bird clock in the kitchen ticks. I am the last one standing. There is no one I can call. No one I can tell.

I return to the computer room. We used to have a greeting card software that I would use to design and print cards for birthdays, Father's Day, Mother's Day. (Yes, I always made Krystal a Mother's Day card. No, I never told my mom.) For Dad and Krystal's anniversary, I sometimes composed a small poem in their card. The poem always rhymed. *Your love is divine, a match made by design.* Lucinda Script. A clip art image of a rose on the front.

The red dot blinks on the screen. Moves forward one block, then pauses. A stoplight. Where is she headed? What is the punch line to this joke? My cell phone rings.

"She's still heading east on Alameda," I say. "Toward Chambers Road. Yeah, just past the library. I'll tell you when she turns."

In my dream, I am with Dad in a house somewhere near the ocean. Though the sky is dark, I can hear the waves crashing against a rocky shoreline. This house is familiar—I think it's the vacation home of one of Krystal's ultra-rich clients who let us stay here on a family trip to Maine. There is a wall of windows, nautical-themed decor. But where is everyone? I look over at Dad, and he is holding a baby, his baby. Here, Dad says, take care of your baby brother. I have to go somewhere. He hands me the baby, and I realize he is holding it in the palm of his hand. The baby is wrinkled, like a raisin, and small enough to fit in a spoon. Its skin is cold to the touch, the body flat on one side, amoeba-like. I cup my hands around its body, trying to warm it. Then the baby squirms, and my grip loosens, and it falls. I am afraid I've killed it. Panicked, I get down on my hands and knees, looking for it, barely able to make out more than shapes in the dim light. I find it on the carpet, still alive. I whisper to it that I'm sorry, and I cradle it against me, and then it begins to grow, skin hardening into an exoskeleton, hands elongating into pincers. It scuttles away, and then I wake.

In hindsight, breakups always seem inevitable. Clues present themselves like little breadcrumbs, leading back into the overgrown forest of the past, throwing into relief all the incompatibilities and deceptions, the minor and major betrayals. Every memory: proof.

There are plenty of details I can't remember, including the name of the hotel in Aurora where Krystal finally stopped that night. Where her little red dot paused on the computer screen. How long I waited to see if the red dot would move, or if this was the place it would stay for the night. Still I wonder: did she know we were watching?

When Dad arrived at the hotel, per my directions, he said "thank you" and hung up. I was an obedient daughter after all. I closed the browser window, switched off the computer, turned off the lamps, and checked the locks. I lay in my old bed, in the room with the crucifixes on the wall and the collection of tiny porcelain Limoges boxes Krystal had bought me as a little girl, Limoges boxes that would be destined for Goodwill in the coming months, as I cleaned out my bedroom in the wake of the divorce.

Staring into the dark, I imagined a thousand scenarios. Krystal, tanned and sinewy, green eyes blazing, stepping into the parking lot, ready for a fight, her finger like the barrel of a gun, pointed at Dad's chest. *I wish I'd never met anyone with the last name Rhoades.* Or Dad pulling a gun from the glove box of the Beamer. Or Alejandro—in tight jeans, hair slicked back—punching Dad in the face. Or Dad grabbing Alejandro by the throat. Or Dad crying, pleading, banging on the door of the hotel room until the police arrived and carried him away. But this was not a James Bond movie; there were no explosions, no gunfire, no grand finale. It was just our life.

The illusion that I maintained throughout my childhood—that I could single-handedly keep the peace by following the rules, by always saying the right thing, by doing my chores without anyone having to ask me—was over. Whatever happened between Krystal and Dad was now far beyond my control. The spell had been broken. The clarity was both terrifying and freeing.

Finally, I fell asleep.

In the light of day, the events of the preceding night seemed like a mirage. Dad was still gone, but would soon return, bleary-eyed from his night watch. He would tell me that nothing happened. That she never left the hotel, though he dutifully watched her car in the parking lot. Never picked up her phone, though he called a hundred times. But before Dad returned, I would peer into Sam's old room. The FUCK YOU Sam had carved into the wall with a pocketknife was still there. It now seemed to me to be the only true thing in the house. In *Synecdoche*, a woman named Hazel says: "The end is built into the beginning."

Everything had changed, and yet nothing had changed. If only I had looked a little closer, paid attention to the signs, I might have predicted that one day everything in this house would burst into flames.

Parenting Diary: Pinewood Derby

January 20, 2001—I went to the Cub Scout Pinewood Derby, an event where the boys race cars they make out of a wood model. It was held at the Cottonwood Creek Elementary School gym. The kids were with Matt this weekend. Sam had been in this event for two years, and I had not gone, primarily because I felt it was something that he did with his dad, and I always feel uncomfortable at events with Matt and Krystal. However, I thought it would be important to show Sam I support him. Krystal came with Sam first (Matt showed up later) and she was holding Sam close to her and hugging him while she talked to me. I said hi to Sam and Lauren, who was there with a friend. Sam and Lauren appeared very stiff and uncomfortable with me. Lauren and her friend stayed close to Matt and Krystal the whole time. Sam sat with his Cub Scout group, and I was standing behind his group talking with my friend Carolee. Krystal came up to me and Carolee while we were talking and said in a loud voice that she was so glad I could finally make it to a Pinewood Derby since this was Sam's third one, and I had never been to one before. She said Sam was so excited that his mother could finally make it. I ignored her as I did not want to get caught up in a confrontation with her. She took Carolee away to talk to another woman. Carolee then left to take care of her small son, and Krystal went over to Sam and sat closely next to him on the floor. She started talking to him very closely and quietly while the event took place.

After Carolee left, another mother came up to me and asked me who my child was. When I told her I was Sam Rhoades's mom she appeared confused and asked who Krystal Rhoades was. I told her Krystal Rhoades was my ex-husband's wife, and I was Sam's mother. She said, Oh, I see Krystal at the school all the time, and she is always talking about how she takes her daughter Lauren to tennis lessons and how involved she is with Sam. She said Krystal was on the Cottonwood Creek PTO yearbook committee and PTO dinner dance committee. She then said how wonderful it must be for me to have a stepmother who was so involved and nice to the kids. I was starting to feel upset, and said it was kind of nice, but Krystal tended to overstep the boundaries of being a stepmother, and I had a hard time with that. I said since I work full time in Lakewood, it's difficult for me to volunteer a lot of my time to the school. I started feeling like I was going to cry and excused myself to leave the room.

The woman followed me out, and started saying how she was so sorry she upset me, she didn't understand the situation, and since Krystal didn't work anymore, she probably didn't have that much to do, and that was why she was volunteering in the school a lot lately. She said, But you know, kids always have that special bond with their mother, and they know who their mother is. At this point, I was outside the school and I broke down and said, I'm not sure about that. My kids are refusing visitation with me now. The woman started crying and said, "Oh my God, this is awful. I am so sorry." The woman's husband came out and said the final races were on. We went back to the gym and the races were over. I saw Sam and Lauren and her friend and Matt and Krystal, who were about ten feet away from me, get their coats and start leaving the gym as a group. None of them looked at me or said goodbye. The woman who was with me was appalled at this bizarre family dynamic. I started crying and said I had to go. Sam came running back into the gym and came over to me and gave me a hug and said, "Bye, Mom." I realized that I shouldn't have said anything to this woman, who I don't even know, but she struck such a chord that I couldn't stop. I don't know if I can go to events with the kids if Matt and Krystal are there.

On the day of the Pinewood Derby, I enter my old elementary school for the first time since leaving fifth grade. Here, in the gym of Cottonwood Creek Elementary I reluctantly placed my hands in Connor C.'s sweaty palms and learned how to square dance. Here, I sat cross-legged on the floor and watched open-mouthed as the D.A.R.E. actor in the giant vulture costume told us that marijuana was a gateway drug. Here, I stood in front of the sea of my classmates, incorrectly spelling "lightning" as "L-I-G-H-T-E-N-I-N-G" at the school spelling bee. Here, I played dodgeball, and dressed up in a poodle skirt for the sock hop, and performed a choreographed dance—choreographed by Krystal—to a Backstreet Boys song in the school talent show.

The gym is smaller, the drinking fountains shorter than I remember, though I know for certain that nothing has changed but me. Race car in hand, Sam folds into the sea of boys in blue uniforms, yellow neckerchiefs. When I spot my mother, her eyes wide and searching, I shrink behind my stepmother and father, glue my gaze to the floor. If I could choose a superpower, it would be invisibility. I want to disappear.

The Pinewood Derby lasts no more than a couple hours. The whole event barely registers in my memory. And yet now, two decades later, I return to this place through my mother's eyes. I thought I knew this place but I didn't. I thought I was big, but I was still so small, easily tricked, fearful. This is what I remember now of that time: the fear. I am so much bigger now. I am no longer afraid. *Mom*, I want to say, *I know you are my mother. And I always knew you were my mother. I love you.*

Mirror, Mirror on the Wall

I have never felt more beautiful than I do now, sitting in this swivel chair, staring at my face in a movie star's mirror, the kind framed with brightly lit bulbs. Behind me, the stylist teases out my bob cut into a dandelion puff and encases my head in a cloud of hair spray that settles like sticky pollen on my skin. Next to me, my new stepmother undergoes her own beauty treatment: hot rollers, back comb, tease out, hair spray. Our faces are powdered, dabbed, brushed. We're having a girls' day out; today we are allies in the pursuit of beauty.

"See?" she says. "It's fun to be pretty."

The Glamour Shots stylist swipes my eyelashes with mascara, and like magic, my eyes seem suddenly larger. They're blue like Dad's, with flecks of gray and green. They glitter like tiny oceans, reflecting the mirror's light. My blonde hair comes from Dad's side too. Even Mom says I look like his sister, my Aunt Mina, though she predicts that my hair will darken as I age. "No, it won't!" I tell her, refusing to relinquish my golden hair. Already, I have learned the ways in which beauty and lightness are intertwined.

The stylist applies dabs of rouge to my cheeks, creating the illusion that I have just come in from the cold. The face in the mirror belongs to someone else now, someone more outgoing, less afraid of making a mistake, someone who thinks it's fun to be pretty. She bats her long eyelashes back at me like a Disney princess.

Glamour Shots is inside Park Meadows Mall, tucked between

Claire's and a pet shop where Mom thinks the animals are mistreated. Bubbly pop music floats through the air. Overhead, there is a TV where you can see your photos and pick out the ones you like in real time. The stylist shows me all the different shades of lipstick, arranged like flowers in a bouquet. I pick out a light pink. Krystal chooses a deep red. Her thin hair is teased so high it looks like cotton candy.

"Look at us," she says, squeezing my waist and pulling me to her. "Like mother and daughter." I file this moment in the category of things I won't ever tell Mom.

Our Glamour Shots package includes two outfits and two poses. For the first photo, I pick out a denim jacket and a floppy brimmed hat with a big sunflower pinned to the front. My attempt at a coy smile looks more like a gap-toothed grin, head tilted to one side, my hands popping out the collar of my jacket. With the Glamour Shots soft focus applied, my skin is smooth as plastic.

Krystal and I pose together for the second shot. This one doesn't involve outfits, but elastic tube tops which won't be visible in the photo. We kneel and the stylist drapes a fluffy pink feather boa in front of us at chest level, creating the illusion that we are naked, floating in a luxurious pool of feathers. I don't like the exposed feeling of wearing the tube top, of my bare shoulder pressed against her bare arm. She wraps her arm around my waist and squeezes. Her acrylic nails press into my skin. I am beginning to understand the way she moves through the world, touching hands, kissing cheeks, squeezing shoulders. I don't like kissing her on the lips the way she insists we do, but I'm getting used to it. Her attention is like a warm spotlight shining on you. When it's gone, you're standing alone on a dark stage.

When I bring the photos home to Mom, she stares at them silently, as if willing the small squares to burst into flames.

"Do you like them?" I ask. We're sitting at the kitchen table, which is scratched and stained from various craft projects gone wrong. She purses her lips, looking from the sunflower hat to the feather boa. I study her face, looking for clues. I've become attuned to her emotions, the way they vibrate beneath the surface of her skin like a taut string ready to snap. I look from the mole on her right cheek to her dark eyes, to her nose which she says looks like George Washington's in profile. Her expression hardens, and for a moment I am afraid she will cry.

"You're a beautiful girl," she tells me. "The most beautiful in the whole world. You know that, right?"

"I guess," I say, knowing already that there are different kinds of beauty, different tiers. Cinderella, for example, is beautiful when she's scrubbing floors, but she's even more beautiful when she's wearing a ball gown. You can tell by the way people look at her.

"I like natural photos of you best, though. Where you look like yourself." Her eyes search mine, as I search hers. Something has broken in them, some fresh disappointment.

"I know," I say, wishing I had hidden the photos away in a drawer. Mom likes to say she is a *natural* woman. When she puts on makeup for work, she pokes around a bag of sample-sized tubes of rouge and cracked eyeshadow palettes. She wears flowy skirts and silver jewelry. Mom thinks *she* spends too much time on her appearance, says *she* is *vain*. We avoid saying Krystal's name.

"I can't help but think about JonBenét Ramsey when I look at you dressed up like this. It makes me sad. It's not right for little girls to wear makeup. Little girls are supposed to play and not worry about how they look."

I know JonBenét from her photos on the news. She's a girl my age—or *was*, before her murder—with pale skin in a fluffy pink dress. A tiny princess with a tiara on her yellow ringlets. In the photos they show, her skin is as smooth and airbrushed as mine is in the Glamour Shots. I wonder if Mom is telling me that beauty—the kind that involves hair spray and makeup—is dangerous, even lethal.

Decades later I will read the letter that Mom writes to Dr. Katz, who, during this time, is conducting a parenting time evaluation for our family. Mom will write, *You should have seen the photos. They made her look like a teenager.*

She doesn't want to hurt my feelings, so she frames the photo of me in the sunflower hat and puts it on the mantle, but hides it behind my new second grade school photo, which features my mismatched front teeth and crooked bangs. Sometimes, I'll move my Glamour Shot to the front, only to discover that days later, it's been hidden again.

Makeup, lighting, hair spray, the perfect angle, a soft filter: these are the beauty secrets of Glamour Shots. A manipulated moment, captured on film. At Dad's house, the photo of Krystal and me is framed, placed on the antique vanity in my bedroom. You might mistake the blonde woman and the blonde child for mother and daughter, if you didn't know better.

In this house, decorated with antiques and oil paintings, there are certain standards of being, of beauty. In this house, my bedroom walls are painted purple; the bedspread is a butter yellow. A slender silver crucifix hangs on the wall above a small wooden desk. Krystal has arranged this room for the girl who lives here half the time, the girl in the Glamour Shots photo. This girl collects tiny porcelain boxes, reads *Dear America* diaries, watches her stepmother attentively as she curls her eyelashes, teases her hair.

"Lauren loves that I dress up," Krystal will tell Dr. Katz in their interview. "She wants her hair and nails done. Lauren wants to be like me."

At Mom's house, the standards are relaxed. The beds may not be made. There may be golden retriever hair on the carpet. My bedroom here is painted lime green, the bedside table bright pink. The color scheme is aggressively happy, upbeat, childlike. The girl who lives here wears overalls and baggy T-shirts, collects penguins, and reads every single book in the *Little House on the Prairie* series. On the doorframe of this bedroom hangs a mezuzah that the girl made in Hebrew school, the tiny prayer folded and tucked inside.

Over the years, each bedroom accumulates more stuff, the extra detritus of living two lives. The girl bifurcates, refracts, doubles back on herself. She is mutable, reflecting whatever world is around her.

In his final parenting report, Dr. Katz will write that one of the girl's bedrooms is "too formally finished" and the other is "too unfinished." He will say that the girl should be encouraged to define herself through what she puts in her room, what she hangs on the walls. I remember talking with Dr. Katz and showing him my bedrooms. I remember his black hair and small, round spectacles, and how he nodded intently and asked me questions which I did not know how to answer. "The report is not intended to be read by the children," Dr. Katz will write. But I will read it, years later when I am no longer a child. The sensation is like seeing oneself as a specimen through the eyes of a highly trained scientist. Like reading a fairy tale about one's own life. In that report, I am Goldilocks, except everything is always too hot or too cold, too soft or too hard, too big or too small. Nothing is just right.

At Mom's house, I play dress-up. Dress-up is not about looking beautiful, though it can be. It's not about the *doing* but the *being*. I like to transform into someone other than myself. I do mundane things—dancing in front of the TV while my brother Sam is watching cartoons, playing with the dog, pouring myself a glass of apple juice—all while wearing too-big high heels and a sequined dress.

Dress-up always begins with the battered plastic tub with rope handles, the one we keep in the basement, and which overflows with polyester, tulle, and sequins. A blue tutu edged in silver trim from my first and only ballet recital. A clown's wig. A tattered sun hat. Mostly, the bin is filled with Mom's old castaway clothes, which she says are "hideous," and "Can you believe I wore that?"

To me, these items are magical and so familiar that I could identify them by touch alone. A floaty pink chiffon bridesmaid dress from the early eighties with see-through sleeves and a rip in the armpit. A pilling polyester maxi dress with floral embroidery, once worn with wooden platform heels. A pair of scuffed red leather flats (which I will one day wear to high school when I finally grow into them). A sequined long-sleeved shirt whose matching skirt has been lost to time. A shiny blue sheath dress with puffy sleeves that Mom once wore to an office Christmas party.

These dresses intrigue me; they are secret clues to Mom's past, the person she was before I existed. I wonder why she bought these clothes, which are bolder and more feminine than anything in her closet now. I imagine her wearing the pink chiffon dress as she applies lipstick in the bathroom mirror, holds a glass of wine, dances in a crowd of people. From old photos, I know her hair was once long, cascading down her shoulders in thick, dark waves. Now it is cropped short. Did she feel beautiful in these clothes? Did she feel like herself?

"Well, it's all downhill from here," Krystal declares walking through the door from the garage. I am flying down the slippery carpet stairs in my sock feet.

"Downhill to where?" I ask. I give her a dry kiss. Her leather coat smells like perfume, hair spray, and winter air. She sits on a step to take off her high-heeled boots. I notice they're almost exactly like Denise Richardson's, whose husband drives a brand-new Hummer and coaches Sam's football team. Sam, at nine years old, is the star running back of the Titans. He pukes before every game, a symptom of anxiety that will persist until his freshman year of high school when he finally quits.

"Downhill to old age," she says with mock self-deprecation. We both know that she knows she's still pretty. "First, these lovely crow's feet show up around my eyes. And now, the guy at the Lancôme counter tells me my skin is dry and aging. So, of course, I had to spend a fortune on these." She holds up a bag filled with tiny jars and vials.

"You're not old," I say. "You don't look a day over thirty." She likes when I say this, even though we both know it's not true. I've noticed how her eyelids look thin and crinkly when she puts on eyeshadow.

"Thanks, pumpkin." I turn to run upstairs, back to my room, but she stops me. "Come here for a second."

I approach, close enough to smell the black coffee she drank and the Listerine strip she ate to cover it up. She's studying my face with a look of concern.

"What is it?" I ask.

"We need to do something about this unibrow," she says, touching the space between my eyebrows with an acrylic fingernail.

I reach up to touch my face. Horrified, I feel soft little hairs growing there.

"I'll take you to get it waxed this weekend," she says. "Before it gets any worse."

I scramble up the steps and run to the bathroom mirror. She's right. Delicate sprigs of dark hairs arch toward one another. I picture them marching steadily together, forming a hairy caterpillar above my eyes. I hate her for pointing out another defect, like the patch of dry skin in the hollow of my neck, or the little bumps on my upper arms. Once I see these parts of me, I can't un-see them.

In his bedroom Sam is pacing back and forth, trying to crack the joints in his neck. I watch him as he walks around his room, stepping around his open backpack, his piles of clothes and books. He juts his head in and out like a chicken. He started doing this a few weeks ago and hasn't stopped.

"Why do you keep doing that? You're going to hurt yourself," I say, leaning against his doorframe. His room here is decorated in a nautical theme, with a red-and-blue quilt and wooden sailboats mounted on the walls. Though I would never ask her, I wonder why Krystal settled on this decorating scheme, since Sam has never been sailing and we live in a landlocked state.

"No, I'm not," Sam replies, still moving his neck. "It feels good." He stops suddenly, looks at me. "Did you hear that? Did you hear it pop?" I roll my eyes.

"You look like an ostrich," I say. I feel annoyed with him, knowing that he'll never have to wax his eyebrows or shave his legs, or worry that his bra strap is showing.

When Dad comes home, I tell him I'm getting my unibrow waxed.

"What are you talking about? You don't have a unibrow," he says examining my forehead under the hanging light in the kitchen. He grips my chin in one hand and rotates my face from side to side. Above us, the bird clock chirps Carolina wren: seven o'clock.

"Yes, I do. See?" I point to the dark hairs which I will never not see. I need them gone. He looks over at Krystal. Her hands are in mitts and she's removing a Costco lasagna from the oven.

"You know she's genetically predisposed," she says, shutting the oven with her hip. "She'll have to start at some point." Dad pretends not to know what—or who—she's talking about, but I know he just doesn't want to get her started. If we both avoid mentioning Mom, then maybe she'll forget that my mother and all my dark-haired relatives exist.

Years earlier, Dr. Katz had noticed the way my father deferred to his new wife, how he "gave up what appeared to be very good parenting instincts" in her presence. He called this dynamic "a ticking time bomb." He predicted that unless something changed, "the children" would be "placed in compromising positions."

"But she's only twelve," he says. He loosens his tie as if undoing a noose. His defenses are weakening by the second, and Krystal and I know it. She removes the lasagna's foil top, puts it back in the oven, and sets the timer for ten more minutes. Then she calls up the stairs for Sam to set the table.

"Please, Dad? It's not that big a deal," I say, even though it's actually a huge deal. I can't bear the thought of keeping my unibrow for another day.

"If you say so, dolly. I'm jealous of anyone that can grow hair," he says, reciting his favorite bald-headed dad joke, and ruffles a hand on my head.

I'm not sure when it happened, exactly. All I know is that one day I woke up and my stepmother had filled the refrigerator with single-serving containers of low-fat, sugar-free yogurt. They are like little plastic soldiers, stacked six deep and three high, their blue lids glinting in the refrigerator's bright beacon of light. They come in a rainbow of flavors: vanilla bean, key lime, mango, banana cream pie.

Once upon a time, the pantry overflowed with peanut butter crackers, Chicken Biskits, Cheez Whiz, Fig Newtons, packages of ramen, and boxes of After Eights. Now there are no snacks, only the essentials: cans of tuna and tomato sauce, jars of olives and sugar-free jelly, boxes of angel hair pasta, bags of croutons and seasoned salad toppings. No more home-baked banana bread. No more drumsticks and ice cream sandwiches in the deep freezer, only giant bags of frozen salmon fillets and chicken breasts.

I am so hungry. Sometimes, when I'm alone in the house, I stand in front of the refrigerator door. Open. Close. Open. Close. I'm looking for something that I already know isn't there.

On weekends, the bird clock taunts me, counting down the hours between meals. In the in-between times, I roam the house, looking for things I want to eat. I can't stomach another yogurt, and tuna makes my stomach turn. At least there are clementine oranges. I eat them five or six at a time. I down sugar-free Crystal Light lemonade made from packets I find in the cupboard. The only marginally interesting food in this house is a giant bucket of Red Vines—Krystal's favorite candy—which sits on top of the fridge. I eat two, maybe three at a time, trying to convince myself that I'm satisfied. But I'm not convinced. Nothing here satisfies me.

Sam tells me he can't stand it here. Most of the time, he's grounded. He forgets to take out the trash, refuses to clean up his room. He can't play video or computer games, can't leave the house to see friends. The TV is in a locked cabinet, and only Krystal has the key. He spends his summer afternoons riding his unicycle up and down the street, plucking hard green apples from the neighbor's tree, and eating them with a pocketknife.

"Can you please not ride with the knife?" I ask him. "If you fall, you'll stab yourself."

"Who cares," he says, riding past me.

I know how you feel, I want to say, but I don't say anything. It is easier to believe that I can fix things myself, that I can *fix myself*.

What I don't understand is how *she* is satisfied, how she is ever not hungry.

Krystal has changed as drastically as our refrigerator and pantry. A few years ago, she started her own garden and landscaping business. Most days, she wears khaki shorts and a T-shirt with her company logo on it, pulls her thin hair back into a ponytail, which she threads through a ball cap. She doesn't bother with acrylic nails now that her hands are calloused from manual labor. She's always been athletic, but now she's whittled down. Her arms are sinewy and tanned to a burnt umber. When she's not working, she's outside in a bikini top transplanting, deadheading, trimming, watering, mowing, transforming our suburban yard into a series of lush gardens that need constant maintenance.

In the summers, I work with her part-time along with a few stay-at-home moms whose sons once played football with Sam. We pull purslane and chop back thick stands of catmint, water thirsty pots of petunias, haul sacks of soil and mulch. She pays us ten dollars an hour in cash, more than what I make at Panera Bread.

At first her clients were regular rich people, the ones with the nicer, newer houses in our neighborhood. But now she's moved up and out of Cherry Creek Vista North and into the estates of Denver's wealthy and well-connected. She tells me her clients prefer having a crew of cute white ladies working their lawns over Mexican guys who don't speak English. Among them are a venture capitalist with an antique car collection and the owner of the largest chain of sporting goods stores in Colorado. Their houses have fountains, pools, horse stables, koi ponds. She knows all the gate codes. I've never seen the owners of these mansions, though I have the eerie feeling that they've seen me on their security monitors.

Work days start early with a light breakfast. For her, that means a low-fat yogurt and black coffee. For me, that means two pieces of thin-sliced toast with sugar-free jelly. Around noon, we pause to eat lunch in the car before heading to the next job site. She opens a single-serve container of low-fat yogurt. Drinks more coffee from her thermos. Says she can't eat when it's hot. I could eat an entire pizza. A whole chocolate cake, like the one the fat kid in *Matilda* was forced to eat in front of the whole school. We've been moving nonstop since 7 a.m., but I pretend that I'm satisfied with the peanut butter and jelly sandwich and baby carrots I packed this morning. I want it to be enough, but it is never enough. By the end of the day, I am lightheaded, sunburnt, exhausted.

Dinner is the only time she allows herself to really eat, though she makes a performance out of consumption, bragging about how many bags of mulch she lifted that day, how many shrubs she planted. I understand that the harder she works, the more permission she has to eat. I start to see food in this way too. What has my body done today to deserve these calories? For dinner, she makes rich food: creamy pastas, meatloaf, salads slathered with Thousand Island dressing. This feels, somehow, perverse. She and Dad drink cheap red wine or vodka with lite cranberry juice. If Sam is grounded, she won't let him eat with us, making him cook his own boxed macaroni.

She is shrinking, and I am expanding. "All my pants are too big," she says in mock sadness. "I'm as flat-chested as a twelve-year-old boy," she complains, clutching at her chest.

Meanwhile, my jeans are tightening. My limbs, which have always been knobby and too long for my body, are filling out. Even my hair grows unruly. Every day, I blow dry and straighten it to hide the curls that sprang up in middle school. As her body hardens, mine softens. When I look in the mirror, an unbearably round face stares back at me. Even when I pluck my eyebrows, apply eyeliner, mascara, blush, and concealer, I can't see the face I once saw in the Glamour Shots mirror. Never have I felt uglier, and more desperate to be beautiful.

Movies and fairy tales have taught me that the young are more beautiful than the old, that stepdaughters should be more beautiful than their stepmothers. But next to her tanned and angular body, I feel pale, cartoonish, outsized.

When Mom tells me I am beautiful, I choose not to believe her. I fail to recognize her unconditional terms as a precious gift, shrugging them off like platitudes. Instead, I work hard to meet the conditions of my stepmother's approval, her fickle love. The time bomb is ticking, nearly ready to blow.

Maybe if I lived here full time, I could learn to like black coffee. I could stay outside in the sun and forget about food. I could whittle myself down into what I used to be—a child. But as soon as I get to Mom's house, relief overwhelms me. There is food there, all our favorite snacks. I eat Oreos dunked in milk, mint chocolate chip ice cream, brown sugar Pop Tarts. But it is always too much. I can never find the balance between underfed and overstuffed. And no matter how much I eat, the hunger always returns.

Mom's hair is its own character in our family drama. For as long as I can remember, she has complained about her untamable hair, its coarse texture, the way it defies gravity and anti-frizz sprays. Her ponytail is the circumference of a fist. She can go two weeks without washing her hair and you'd never know, the natural oils soaking back into her voluminous mane. She is forever growing her hair out, or lopping it off in frustration, agonizing over whether to color her roots or let them go gray, searching for the perfect stylist who can magic her hair into something it wasn't meant to be.

"I hate my hair. I wish I had hair like yours," Mom tells me all the time. My hair may be easier to control, but I also dislike it in its natural state: curly, frizzy, asymmetrical. Her whole life, Mom has searched for the secret thing that will make her hair *good*. Maybe this is why she indulges me in my own quest for perfect hair. Throughout high school, she takes me to nice stylists to get my hair cut, fills the space under the bathroom sink with hair creams and oils, diffusers and flat irons, pays for highlights when my blonde hair begins to darken, even caves when I beg to get my hair chemically straightened, a process which leaves it brittle and dull. *If only . . . , if only . . .* we mutter in front of our mirrors.

When I learn how to French braid, Mom lets me practice on her. "Just get it off my neck," she says, as if her hair is a tightening boa constrictor. She sits cross-legged on the floor in the living room, propped up against the couch. I sit behind her, dividing her dark hair into thick strands, weaving one strand into another, into another. In his report, Dr. Katz had written that I was most affected by my mother's "paralysis," that my "inhibited anxiety" mirrored her own.

But in this moment, there is no anxiety, no inhibition. We are mother and daughter, tribal animals, grooming one another, expressing love in the most primal of ways.

"Don't be afraid to make it really tight," she tells me, looking straight ahead. "I want this to last."

"Beauty takes pain," I say, cheerfully. This is my joke, what I tell my friends when we experiment with hair removers or pose for homecoming photos in uncomfortable high heels. We laugh because it's the truth.

Mom lets out a groan as I pull back the hair behind her ears.

"Sorry," I say, "too tight?"

"Nope, just keep going."

When I finish the braid, I secure it with an elastic hair tie, step back to appraise my handiwork.

"It looks good!" I say. "Sleek, like a fish." Mom pats her head gently. I hand her a mirror so she can see the back.

"You really got it this time," she says. "It feels good to have it up."

"Mom, your head looks like a stegosaurus," Sam says, walking by. We laugh. Her hair is so thick that the braid does form a stegosaurus-like ridge down the middle of her head. She leaves it anyway.

One day, I too, will get fed up with my hair, will get tired of its weight on my neck. At that point, I will be living in another state, no longer landlocked. I will go to the beauty school down the street where they charge fifteen dollars for a haircut, and tell the student stylist that I want her to shave my head. "Are you sure?" she'll ask. When I assure her that I am, she'll go looking for her instructor. I'll wonder, *how hard is it to shave a head?* The instructor will come over with clippers. I will watch as clumps of hair fall to the ground, will feel the pleasant buzz of metal against my scalp. A couple other students will gather around the instructor, attentive to this impromptu lesson in how to uniformly shave a woman's head. I feel as if some ritual shearing is taking place, as if the woman wielding clippers is a high priestess and I am her sacrificial lamb, as if this moment will divide my life into a *before* and an *after*. When she finishes, she will brush the loose hairs from my neck, unsnap the cape. "Take a look," she'll say. I will tilt my head from one side to the other, meeting my eyes in the mirror, inspecting the newly visible tops of my ears, the bare nape of my neck. I will see my face, and I will recognize the person looking back at me.

Children of Divorce

I was swimming in grief the year I met Antoine, my first husband. It was the year that my father's and Krystal's divorce was finalized; the year that my best friend Sarah's brother Travis—the same age as my own brother—committed suicide just days before his seventeenth birthday; the year I left to study abroad in Argentina. I had just turned twenty.

I felt I should be celebrating the end of my father's second marriage to my stepmother, the end of a relationship ruled by fear, dishonesty, and manipulation. Their home (which had been my home, too, for the past twelve years) was emptied now and on the market. That spring, I tossed the contents of my childhood closet and drawers—old clothes, mementos, heirlooms—into giant garbage bags which Dad then dropped off at Goodwill. I didn't know what happened to most of the other stuff in the house—the mahogany antiques, gilt-framed oil paintings, the handmade quilt Phyllis had made for me. I didn't care. *Good riddance.* Divorce, I thought, would release me from my stepmother's torments and my father's complacency. Instead, I felt empty, numb.

While divorce is like a death, it is not death. I could not stomp on the grave of the bad witch, because the witch—my ex-stepmother—was still alive and well. From what I had heard, she was fit and tan and had a new boyfriend—maybe the one she had cheated on my father with, or maybe someone new. The freedom I found in the wake of her departure was costly, unsatisfying. I couldn't help but feel that Krystal was the real winner here, while the rest of us would be left choking on her dust for years to come.

Dad was like the survivor of a shipwreck, marooned in a one-bedroom apartment that he'd crammed with the remnants of his former four-bedroom life: the overstuffed eggplant-colored leather couch that had once anchored our large family room, the mahogany sleigh bed he'd shared with Krystal, and the few things that were his and his alone—books and rock specimens and framed Ansel Adams posters. Visiting him was like walking into a time capsule, each artifact a painful reminder of what we'd lost. I couldn't bear to stay much longer than an hour or two.

In retrospect, I was grieving a loss so immeasurable that I didn't know how to parse it into words. Plus, to admit to my own private sufferings seemed indulgent in the face of Sarah's loss, the worst loss I could imagine. Sarah had lost her brother. Her parents had lost their only son. I had lost a shitty stepmom. As I had learned in algebra class, losing a negative is equivalent to adding a positive.

That summer, I mourned for Sarah and her family, for Travis. The sadness gutted me, turned me helpless and afraid. When my brother and I went hiking in the mountains of southern Colorado a few weeks after the funeral, I made us turn around when the trail got too steep and rocky. *I don't want to die before I get to Argentina*, I told him. *And I can't handle the thought of you dying, too.* I wasn't being hyperbolic. I really was afraid to perish before I got the chance to escape.

And then my summer turned abruptly to winter. In July, I arrived in the Southern Hemisphere. I stood in the Buenos Aires Ezeiza airport, surrounded by suitcases and a couple dozen American exchange students who looked as jetlagged and bewildered as I felt. Next to me was a tall, lanky guy wearing a bright red University of Wisconsin hoodie.

"Let me guess," I said, "study abroad?"

"How can you tell?" he replied in an accent that was not American, let alone Midwestern. I pointed to the giant badger on his hoodie. He smiled, revealing a set of charmingly crooked teeth.

"You're from Wisconsin?" I asked, though I doubted it. I knew my own voice made it clear that I was from somewhere in the middle of America, though I had left all traces of my own school allegiances behind. That, I believed, was the point of escape—to wipe the slate clean.

"From France, but I go to University of Wisconsin. I'm an international student there."

"You're an exchange student twice removed," I said. He laughed. We shook hands. Lauren from Colorado; Antoine from Normandy by way of Wisconsin.

Even through my exhaustion, I felt a spark of curiosity about this Frenchman. Maybe it was the way his eyebrows dipped together into an unmistakable unibrow. Or the way his chin jutted forward at a jaunty angle, so that in profile, his face had somewhat the shape of a crescent moon. Or that his body seemed to be all limbs and knees and elbows. Or that somehow, this collection of eclectic features seemed perfectly balanced by an underlying athletic grace and a confident, disarming sense of humor.

I had fantasized about meeting a handsome Argentine, a *porteño*—someone who would show me the city, who would speak Spanish with me, someone who wouldn't recognize the miserable sameness I felt inside, the feeling that had propelled me to get as far away from home as I possibly could. But here was Antoine. He was different from anyone I had ever met. In fact, all the students and faculty were charmed by him, the lone French student in the *yanqui* study abroad program, the guy who could juggle a soccer ball and outmaneuver anyone on a bike polo court, who bulldozed his way through the Spanish language by inserting a mixture of French and English words whenever he got stuck. The more time I spent with Antoine, the more I felt that he was the fix to everything inside me that was broken. For so long, I had been a split person—torn between my divorced parents—and yet in his eyes I was whole.

Antoine's parents were divorced, too, a fact I learned over a bottle of wine we shared inside a warm Buenos Aires bar on a bitterly cold August night. I was thrilled that I could legally order and drink wine inside a bar, though I was still below the legal American drinking age. This, in turn, amused Antoine, the way every part of American drinking culture amuses the French. The things I had once accepted as normal were beginning to melt away, revealed to be nothing more than a set of arbitrary cultural practices. And yet divorce appeared to be an international mainstay. My Argentine host mom was divorced, and her teenage son divided his time between her house and his father's. Most of the time, Juan was there when I arrived home after class, watching TV or practicing his saxophone. And then some of the time he was not. I could never quite catch on to the rhythm of their custody schedule, and I wondered if that's how my friends had felt about me growing up, when they would call the wrong house looking for me.

Antoine's parents had split when he was in his early teens and were now both remarried. Back then, I didn't know the statistics that show that partners who both have divorced parents are 200 percent more likely to get divorced themselves. (In couples where one spouse comes from a divorced home, the risk of divorce is only 50 percent higher.) But we were on our first date, and the concept of marriage was still a distant theoretical phenomenon. His mother and stepfather lived in Normandy, and his father, stepmother and their young daughter were traveling the world on a sailboat. Our childhoods had been vastly different, and yet the simple fact that we were both "children of divorce" entering into our first long-term relationship allied us, gave us a roadmap for the kind of relationship we would pursue, the insecurities we would share.

When we first started dating, Antoine talked constantly about the shoestring motorcycle trip he planned to take across South America after the end of our first study abroad semester. The trip was his dream and the main reason he had chosen to come to Argentina in the first place, inspired by a combination of Che Guevara hero-worship and a warm nostalgia for the motorbike trips he had taken with his father in Morocco. Midway through the semester, I, too, caught the "Che" bug after Antoine convinced me to watch *The Motorcycle Diaries*. Perhaps it was the swoon-worthy sight of Gael García Bernal in a leather jacket, or the fact that we were curled up in Antoine's twin bed, his long limbs entwined in mine, watching the movie on the screen of his laptop. I felt warm and protected in his arms, and at the end of the movie, when he kissed my neck and invited me to join him on his epic adventure, I agreed without hesitation. The question alone was more romantic than any marriage proposal I could imagine.

"Who is picking up the freight for this vacation?" my father fired off in a late-night email when he learned about my summer plans. "You sure seem to do things your way. I cannot wait until you graduate and have to get a J-O-B like the rest of us stiffs." I did not remind him that ever since the divorce, when he had stopped being able to contribute to my college expenses, Mom and Cecil had been the ones "picking up the freight." I also did not "nail him to his hypocritical cross," as Sam advised me to do. I simply replied that I would be graduating in just over a year, and that he could wait until then to revel in my working a thankless underpaid job while living with three roommates in a dingy apartment. I was a continent and a lifetime removed from his *800-pound gorilla* lectures and my evil ex-stepmother, and now I had a boyfriend with a motorcycle. I was untouchable.

My mother, on the other hand, was afraid for my safety, but willing to accept that my choices were my own. In an email, she wrote:

> You and Antoine can be as safe as possible, but you can't control other cars. That is why I must insist that you wear a helmet. I know you've

already made up your mind to do this, so can you please ease your mother's anxiety over this and tell me you will wear a helmet, jacket, and long pants? Please buy the right gear and let me know how much it is and I will put extra money in your account.

To ease my mother's anxiety (and embrace my new carefree, edgy persona), I bought a leather jacket and a shiny black helmet. Antoine bought a helmet with a cartoonish eagle head painted on the back. "Get it?" he asked, chuckling to himself. "America, fuck yeah!" I covered my face with my hands in mock shame. He enjoyed poking fun at American patriotism and sometimes liked to tell strangers that he was from Paris, Texas. As it turned out, I was the one who would spend many hours contemplating that ironic symbol of American freedom while my ass went numb on the back of his motorcycle.

We left Buenos Aires in December, Antoine driving an old Honda motorcycle he had purchased from an auto mechanic, and me clinging to his torso. We traveled west across Argentina, crossed the Andes, drove up the desert coast of Chile, and into the high plateau of Bolivia, the cartoon eagle mocking me through driving rain and scorching heat. My own version of freedom was not brash like an eagle's. It was subtle, delicate. Layer by layer, my interior world had begun to unfurl; the fragile self I had concealed and protected for many years began to emerge. So ubiquitous was the eagle's presence—with its sharp yellow beak and narrowed, slit-like eyes—that after a few weeks, I forgot it was there at all. I forgot, too, that I was living Antoine's dream, not my own.

Midway through our trip, we were in La Paz, Bolivia, in a cramped, dimly lit hostel room. I had spent the last twelve hours vomiting into the toilet after eating unpasteurized ice cream the night before. Antoine had gone out to get me antibiotics, bottled water, and crackers, and then patiently stayed in bed with me while a dubbed version of *The Big Bang Theory* played on TV. I watched him, his eyes glued to the screen as Spanish-accented Sheldon shouted yet another enthusiastic

"Bazinga!" and thought about how much we had already experienced in the short time we'd known each other. Together we had survived flat tires, food poisoning, hunger and dehydration, long days on the open road, and cold drives through pouring rain. Early on in our relationship, he had written me a letter listing all the things he liked about me, from the way my whole face would inexplicably grow red with embarrassment, to my sense of humor, to the color of my eyes. I knew that what I felt toward him then was love—or at least what I imagined love to be—and I knew he must feel the same way.

"Hey, can I tell you something?" I asked.

"Of course," he said, turning his eyes away from the TV to look at my face. I paused, hesitating. I knew I looked horrible in that moment—greasy haired, sickly, my face pale against the hostel's thin, patterned comforter.

"I think I love you."

His expression shifted to a confusing mixture of surprise and fear. He kissed me, then buried his face in my hair so that I couldn't see his eyes.

"You know I really like you. A lot. Like *a lot*, a lot."

"It's okay. You don't have to say it back." I rubbed his back reassuringly. I was disappointed, but not heartbroken. We were still new. I told myself that he showed me love in countless ways. That was enough.

A week later, we were in Sucre, a picturesque colonial town in the southern highlands of Bolivia. After a harrowing time in La Paz, we had decided to splurge here. The night before we had treated ourselves to a fancy meal at—of all places—a French restaurant. And now we were drinking coffee and playing chess at a little café that overlooked the tile roofs of the city below.

"Look," he said, "about what you said in La Paz."

"What did I say?" I asked. I kept my eyes on the chessboard, pretending to be engrossed in my pawn's next move. He hesitated.

"About how you love me."

"Oh, that."

"It's not that I don't love you. I mean I want to love you, and someday I want to *tell* you 'I love you,' but I—I can't right now," he said, breathlessly. We still had not looked up from the chessboard. "My parents loved each other, and then they ended up lying and manipulating each other. I promised myself I wouldn't end up like them. I can't rush things, take risks like that."

I didn't point out that just days earlier he had insisted we go on a downhill mountain bike tour of the aptly named "Death Road" outside La Paz. I had been the careful one then, my hands cramped and white-knuckled as I squeezed the brakes while daredevil Antoine raced ahead, jumping off rocks and purposely skidding his tires close to the edge of the road's gravelly drop-off. He guarded his heart more closely than he did his own body. Perhaps this was the difference between us then. I was ready to give him my whole heart even if I thought that one day it would break.

"I understand," I said. "I promise, I do. But for me, love doesn't mean forever. You can love someone for a summer, or for a lifetime. It's not like I'm asking you to marry me. I'm not trying to rush you. I'm just telling you how I feel now."

"And I'm telling you how I feel," he said. "What happens when I go back to Wisconsin? And you to Colorado? I don't want to feel like we're holding each other back."

"I don't know," I said. Hot tears filled my eyes, and the squares of the chessboard blurred in front of me. "I don't know any more than you."

What did I know then about love? I knew that to love someone, you must trust them. You must be willing to make sacrifices for them out of a spirit of generosity, not bitterness. Antoine and I were willing to make sacrifices, but only if it seemed that the other person was making a sacrifice of similar magnitude. We were obsessed with fairness. On our motorcycle trip, we kept a little pouch for our shared money. The pouch had the word "PANAMA" embroidered on it, a cheap souvenir from a trip Antoine had taken to that country years before, made of colorful cotton and string. Each week, we would withdraw some cash from an ATM, then put an equal amount inside the pouch. "Panama" became a shorthand for our shared money. It worked well, until it didn't.

"Is this a Panama expense?" Antoine might say after dinner.

"You ordered dessert," I might reply, "and I didn't."

"And I bought you those antibiotics the other day."

"And I bought the last tank of gas."

We went around and around, the pouch of cash dangling like a haunted talisman from our necks. And yet the money inside the pouch was not really ours but our parents', though we each found ways of justifying our use of it. I had gotten scholarships and worked as an RA to lighten my mother's financial burden (though she still wired money regularly into my bank account, see above). Antoine had promised his father that he would eventually pay back the "loan" of his college tuition money. We were not independent, not by a long shot. We were privileged barely-adults on a year-long adventure. As my father had caustically pointed out, we were not "picking up the freight," but coasting along on our relative affluence. And still we refused to give freely to one another, guarding jealously what little was ours. Most days, we ate frosted animal crackers for breakfast, slept in tents and dirty hostels, counted our cash, and ignored the forces that had shaped us, that were continuing to shape us.

These arguments repeated and echoed throughout the years. We did stay together. We were long distance while I finished my last year of school in Colorado, post-study abroad, and then when I graduated, I moved into Antoine's cramped but charming student cooperative house in Wisconsin, while he finished his final semester. Then we both moved to DC.

When we were no longer adventuring, but working entry-level office jobs, trying to make a living and find meaning in the new banal reality of adulthood, our disagreements about fairness—who paid which bill, who had last washed the laundry, picked up the groceries, cleaned the kitchen—exhausted me. We did our best to avoid fighting. Fighting was what our parents had done, and we were not our parents. We *refused* to be our parents. Instead of yelling, we grew silent and moody, we retreated deeper and deeper into our own internal worlds, tending privately to our own wounds, just as we had done as children. And wasn't our obsession with fairness a direct response to our childhoods as well? Hadn't we been programmed to make sure our parents had an equal share of us? Hadn't we watched as they'd divided their resources, divided our time, quibbled over custody schedules, counted each hour and expense, communicated via lawyers and intermediaries? We didn't *want* to be them, but this is all that we knew.

Even today, I find myself preoccupied with fairness, though I fight against the impulse now—in my relationships, in my marriage, in myself. Fairness—not to be confused with equality—is a symptom of self-absorption, a small-spiritedness born of division, "division" being a word which shares the same etymological roots as "divorce."

I wondered about the ways our childhoods had affected us. Antoine idolized his father, who was still sailing around the world on a catamaran, ostensibly free. As a teenager, his father had encouraged him to think big and take risks, to leave home, to go to America. He was a jovial, magnetic Anglophile who was constantly joking and playing pranks. I, too, had once idolized my father, but those years were long gone. Divorce had changed me yet again. My dad and Krystal's divorce had stripped down their relationship to its most essential, monstrous core. I still loved my dad, but I also saw his flaws. Father worship was suspect to me. But Antoine saw his own father once every few years, and I knew that it was easier, of course, to worship from afar.

I wondered, too, why Antoine would not let me communicate with his parents, particularly his mother, without his knowledge or consent.

"I don't want you talking about me behind my back," he would say, and he was serious. No emails, greeting cards, or phone calls passed between us without his authorization. His mother lived in Normandy, and there was rarely a reason for us to be in touch without cc-ing our beloved mutual contact. Not until the week she learned we had broken up did she send me a private email, our very last communication. The subject line then read "Confidential."

I, too, was scarred in countless ways. In our post-college years, when we lived in a series of small, under-furnished apartments in DC, I could not eat a meal without inputting the meal's calories into a calorie tracker. I kept the tracker a secret, just as I had kept my late-night binge-eating a secret back in Argentina, when I was sneaking down to my host mother's kitchen late at night, stuffing myself with dry crackers and spoonfuls of apricot jam, anything to distract me from the pain I had left behind on another continent.

In those DC years, I was the skinniest I'd been since early high school. After work, I went for long runs along the Potomac or did Jillian Michaels workout videos, then lay out by our apartment's pool, exposing my flat stomach to the sun, smugly enjoying my newfound willpower. I reveled in the hunger that would come in the evening, when the calorie tracker showed I had an energy deficit. I wanted to become smaller. I wanted control. My journals from that time are filled with entries about food, chastising myself for binging peanut butter, or cheering myself on when I stuck to a low carb meal plan.

Perhaps, too, I seemed needy. And I was. I believed that a romantic relationship would and should fulfill me. All of me, not just a *part*. I sulked when Antoine came home late from bike polo practice, smelling of sweat and cheap beer, hopped up on endorphins. I resented him because I had been at home, friendless and alone, though he hadn't forbade me from making my own plans, my own friends.

And then there was the fact that nearly three years after that night in La Paz, Antoine could still not say he loved me. "*Mi amor*," he called me, "*mon coeur*"—my love, my heart. For us, love was a name, not an action, and I did not know when or if this would ever change. On the phone with Sarah one night, I confessed the fact that we still never said "I love you."

"That's odd, Lauren. That's not good," she said.

"But I know he loves me—he shows me he does. He just can't say it. He is afraid. His parents divorced, you know, and . . ." But my excuses felt stale, and Sarah was not swayed. She was two years into a relationship with a man who both spoke and showed his love, proof that that was possible. How long could Antoine and I continue to blame our parents for our own behavior? Blaming your problems on divorced parents felt cliché, immature. I wondered if Sarah thought that, too.

Later that year, Sarah came to visit me in DC. The three of us took the metro to the grocery store to stock up on food for the week. At the last minute, she threw a gallon of lemonade into the cart. When it came time to carry our groceries back onto the metro, the bag with the lemonade strained at her arm. "Antoine, will you take it?" Sarah asked. "You're stronger than me."

"You wanted the lemonade, so you have to carry it," he said. Sarah laughed, then realized he wasn't joking. She turned to me, eyebrows raised. I shrugged. His statement wasn't cruel, and I could see the logic behind it, but it was unkind. There is fairness, and then there is rigidity. On the walk back to our apartment, Sarah and I each took a handle of the bag, sharing the burden between us.

When Dad and Krystal's marriage finally ended, I remember understanding with a sudden, white-hot clarity how inevitable the end had been all along. The clues were right there, under our noses. How idiotic our past selves looked to me then, groping blindly around the cave of our own ignorance. "You can love rich, just like you can love poor," Krystal had often said. I never stopped to think how that idiom applied to her own love for my father, a love which dissipated right around the same time that it became clear that he was not, nor ever would be, rich.

You can love rich or poor, and you can tote more than you should. Looking back, it seems obvious to me now that my relationship with Antoine was doomed from the start, and not only because of the statistics. I was carrying far more than I should have and slowly collapsing under the weight. I believed that this is what a relationship required.

After about a year in DC, Antoine's visa was due to expire. The company he worked for was small and not able to sponsor a work visa. A green card seemed like the only tenable way for him to stay in the U.S.

"Are you sure you're okay with this?" Antoine asked, when he first broached the topic of marriage.

"Of course," I replied without hesitation. "No matter what happens, I want to do this for you."

"Obviously, I'll pay for all the attorney fees, and handle the paperwork," he said.

"Okay," I said. I held his hand in mine.

I wanted to be generous. I wanted to give this to him. I wanted to carry my share of his burden without expecting anything in return. Without worrying if it was fair. Yet even then, the doubts about our relationship were rising like floodwater. Weeks later, I wrote in my journal:

Marriage is a legal label with a moral code attached, and it makes me want to run. I'm just not ready for the finality of marriage. I'm going to do it so Antoine can continue to live and work here. I'll stay married for the obligatory two years, but I'm not making promises to stay in this relationship.

We wed on a dreary, cold January day in DC. An arbitrary date, a weekday morning. I don't remember the date now. Later, when we were splitting up, I would wonder if the US Customs and Immigration Services official overseeing Antoine's green card case would find this detail suspect, proof that our marriage was a sham. Who gets married in the middle of the week?

On the morning of the court appointment, I dressed in my nicest work outfit: a black pencil skirt and a pink silk blouse I had bought at an upscale consignment store. I wore black tights and black boots, a black down winter coat. I put on knit gloves and tucked my umbrella into my bag. I had told my boss that I had a doctor's appointment.

The DC courthouse loomed gray and monolithic against the gloomy sky. We queued at the front door before entering into a stark, concrete-walled atrium whose sole architectural purpose seemed to be making its visitors feel sad and insignificant. "No one is smiling," I whispered in Antoine's ear, after retrieving my bag from the metal detector.

"Because no one wants to be here," he replied, taking my hand. "Except us."

Except us. I was not so sure about that. In the marriage license division on the fourth floor, I felt anxious and unexpectedly embarrassed. We waited in a lobby for our names to be called, my feet shifting on the stained gray carpet. *It was like a worn-down dentist office lobby*, I later wrote in my journal. I was aware of how young I looked. Sometimes strangers thought I was in high school despite the fact that I was twenty-three. Too young, too immature to get married. But this was not a *real* marriage. Could people tell?

A woman with short gray hair—the officiant—entered the lobby and called our names. In my journal, I described her as a *middle-aged Jewish woman—very business-like, but friendly and trying to lighten the mood.* That phrase—*lighten the mood*—stands out to me now. Had she sensed my discomfort and trepidation? Could she read the regret on my face?

We followed her into the ceremony room. The carpet in here was the color of coagulated blood; an arch of faded silk flowers stood at the front of the room. I wanted to laugh at the cheesiness of this institutional attempt at romantic ambience, which so starkly contrasted with the rest of the building. I was reminded of the cheap hostel where Antoine and I had stayed in a seedy neighborhood of Santiago, Chile, the kind with the option to pay by the hour. When we opened the door to our room, our jaws dropped. The lighting was dim and tinged pink. The walls and ceiling were painted a deep maroon, the headboard was in the shape of a giant heart, and the comforter was a cheap synthetic silk. There were no windows. I didn't want to imagine the deeds that had been done on that bed. Dropping our bags onto the neon pink chairs in the corner, we laughed at our own naïveté, triple-checked the lock on the door, slept fully clothed, and left early the next morning.

No, you could not force romance, just like you could not force someone to tell you that they loved you. Deep down, I think I knew then that the motorcycle trip had been the best part of our relationship, that everything that came after would be an attempt to replicate the same feeling of discovery—discovery of the world and of each other.

We stood under the silk flower arch, holding hands. We had no guests in attendance, as neither of us had told our families what we'd decided to do. At the time, Sarah was the only person who knew that I was getting married, and she was in Michigan. As the officiant led us through the vows, tears welled in my eyes. Antoine smiled at me tenderly. Later he mentioned my tears, how touched he was by them. He thought they were tears of joy, and I didn't correct him. I would never tell him that as I vowed to love and care for my legally wedded husband for as long as we both shall live, I realized that I did not love him anymore, that I could not spend the rest of my life with him. This revelation struck me fully formed; it lodged itself in my guts, innocuous as a kidney stone. The officiant took a photo of us standing beneath the arch. It was our only wedding photo, and later this, too, worried me. Would USCIS be suspicious of a couple with only one poorly lit, slightly crooked wedding photo?

Mom had once told me that on the day of her and Dad's wedding, at the moment when she was to walk down the aisle, she'd had a bad feeling, a desire to turn and run. When she told me this, I wondered if her memory was revisionist. The *bad feeling* seemed like her brain's way of reconciling past events with present circumstances, their obvious incompatibility. Her desire to run from my father would have been a premonition. Eventually, he'd be the one to turn and run from her. Bad feelings on wedding days were the make-believe stuff of Hollywood movies, I had thought until now. Here I was reciting my marriage vows, the bad feeling rising in my throat like acid.

I was nearly the age my mother had been when she and my father married, and I felt as though I knew her in a new way—not as a parent, but as a young woman sharing her life with a man, molding herself to fit the man's world, adjusting herself to his needs. My mother's past had become my emotional compass. I saw how a small, buried seed of doubt could grow a noxious root system, hidden from everyone but yourself. As a child, I wasn't interested in knowing how and why marriages failed; I knew only that they did, that a divorce was like a natural disaster—calamitous and unpredictable. Now I could see that this wasn't the case. There were signs, subtle shifts, fissures. I needed to pay attention to the bad feeling, to trust what it was telling me.

Outside the courthouse, we opened our umbrellas and kissed goodbye. "Goodbye, husband," I said as we parted. "Goodbye, wife," he called back. Then we walked to our separate metro lines and rode to work. I should have told Antoine then how I was feeling. Instead, I tried to ignore the feeling in my gut, pretending it would go away. But the feeling was persistent and painful—I had already chosen my path.

The week before my twenty-fourth birthday, only four months into our marriage, I told him that I wanted to break up. Lying in our shared bed, in our basement apartment, we cried and held each other in the dark. The following week, we had our first interview with the USCIS, the next step in Antoine's green card process. We held hands in that room, bracing each other as we answered the official's questions as honestly as we could, while pretending we were happy newlyweds. As far as the government was concerned, we would continue pretending for the next two years, the minimum amount of time USCIS requires for a marriage to have been made in "good faith."

I want to believe that divorce works like a vaccine, that one small divorce inoculates against the chances of it happening again when the stakes are higher, when children and houses and families are involved. I think it was Cheryl Strayed who once said—tongue in cheek—that second marriages are the best kind of marriages. Strayed claimed a new last name after her divorce from her first husband. "I saw the power of the darkness," she writes in her memoir *Wild*. "Saw that, in fact, I *had* strayed and that I *was* a stray and that from the wild places my straying had brought me, I knew things I couldn't have known before."

I occupied a liminal space after my breakup with Antoine. After a week of staying with Mom and Cecil while Antoine moved his things into a friend's house, I returned to our apartment, to our bed, and felt a sharp loneliness. I missed him. And yet a world of possibility was opening to me. He later sent me an email asking me *why* I wanted to break up, a question that felt impossible to answer truthfully. I responded, saying:

> My real fear is that I'm letting go of the man who cares about me more than anyone in the world in exchange for—what?—nothing? And what if I realize that I made a mistake, and I want this man back and he's gone? But this unknown void is something that I need to explore on my own. I have to take this risk.

I needed the unknown. I was feral, hungry to experience life as an untethered, single person. I was free, but Antoine was in a free fall. Though he had never outright said he loved me, he wrote an email telling me I was the only girl he had ever loved.

"Is there someone else?" he asked me just weeks after he had moved out. "Tell me, for real. I can handle it." We had agreed to meet for pupusas at the El Salvadoran place down the street, though neither of us could touch our food. Our pain hovered over the table like a dense fog.

"No," I said. "There's no one else."

"You're sure," he said. His eyes had a hardened, desperate look to them, and in that moment, I knew that he hated me.

"There's no one else, I promise," I said, meeting his stare.

"God, I wish there was. It would be so much easier if there was."

In the wake of his divorce from Krystal, my dad was unmoored, bereft. I never saw Krystal, but I got the impression that she was just fine. She was free. I resented Krystal's behavior, resented her with every cell in my body, but in a twisted way, I could understand the attraction of cutting off one's past and fashioning a completely new identity. I wanted to be free and new, too.

I emailed Antoine over a month after our awkward pupusa dinner to tell him that he had received some mail at the apartment, and also that I had put in my two weeks' notice at work, and would soon be moving to Mississippi for an AmeriCorps position. In a long reply, Antoine called me selfish. He said the way I had left him wasn't fair, that *he* didn't deserve the pain *I* caused him. He said that *you owe respect to the people that you're with in order to respect yourself.* I read the email on my laptop, in the bedroom we had shared until so recently, the bedroom I would soon be leaving. I felt strangely impervious to his suffering, as though I was reading the words a stranger had written me, as though my body had been drained of its ability to feel empathy. I had already given him more than I owed. There is selfishness, and then there is self-preservation.

In a writing workshop, a classmate who had given me feedback on an essay about my divorced parents asked me about my beliefs around marriage. "From what I understand," she said, "you're happily married now. How did that happen?" Her question was so sincere, so open. And I knew what she was really asking. Her parents were divorced, too; they had split when she was in high school. *How did you overcome this hereditary disease?* She wanted to know. *How do we do it?*

"Maybe I'll write an essay about it," I said, dodging the question. What I didn't say was this: My parents were married eleven years before they split. My father and stepmother were married thirteen. My grandparents were married for nearly twenty. Check back in five years, ten years, a couple decades from now. Check back after we have children. Divorce bides its time.

I often forget about my first marriage and, subsequently, my first divorce. It's one of those little-known facts about myself, an almost-secret that I used to reveal to friends after a few drinks. "I'm a divorcee," I would tell them and watch with satisfaction as their confusion made way to disbelief, wonder. The word itself—*divorcee*—seemed cosmopolitan and in no way connected to the person I really was: someone in their mid-twenties who drank cheap beer and wore thrifted clothes. Afterwards I always felt a little ashamed about my confession, as if I had been bragging about pain, or dishonesty.

Children of divorce, the studies say, "hold a comparatively weak commitment to the norm of lifelong marriage." Well, obviously. We know that divorce was the best option for our parents, no matter how badly they fucked up the aftermath. Still, I do believe that a good, lasting marriage is possible. I also believe that the future is unknowable, that our future *selves* are unknowable. I barely recognize the person I was over a decade ago, the person sitting across from her former lover in the red plastic booth, her uneaten pupusas turning cold and hard on the Styrofoam plate in front of her. How can I assume to know anything about the person I will be ten years in the future? She is a black box, her desires inscrutable. One of my greatest fears is that she will want to run, to destroy the careful balance of my relationship with my husband. Will she cradle our same dear love? Or will she have let the love curdle and sour? I worry that the statistics will inevitably reveal themselves as statistics are known to do. But deeper than fear is trust—I trust my future self, though she is a mystery. I trust her instinct for self-preservation. I trust her more than I trust marriage. I have to. Perhaps what social scientists call the "generational transmission" of divorce is merely a self-protective realism about the unknowable future, about the thousands of ways it might turn out, divorce being among those ways.

I'm now at the age where divorce is spoken about in hushed tones, especially among the married set, as if the mention of it will curse your happiness and stability. Talking frankly about divorce makes married people feel uncomfortable, even though I know plenty of friends who have now divorced their high school and college sweethearts.

A few years ago, I received a call from Sarah while I was on my way to the gym. She was distraught because her parents had told her that they had decided to end their decades-long marriage. I parked the car and sat there while she told me how they had broken the news together, had announced that they'd be selling the house where she had grown up, how her father would be moving to Florida, where he'd always dreamed of retiring. I thought of her old bedroom, where I'd spent many nights, where we made prank phone calls and laughed about the boys we liked. I thought of Travis's room across the hall, which had been left mostly untouched since his death, a shrine to his sixteen-year-old self.

"You've been through this," she said, "you know how this feels." But I didn't really. I didn't know how to grapple with the reality that your parents didn't love each other after a lifetime of believing they did. Stranger still was the fact that Sarah's parents planned to remain friends; no animosity lingered between them. There was no roadmap I could offer my childhood friend, though I wished I could. I was sad for Sarah, for the added logistics she would have to navigate at holidays, for the new challenges of a more complicated family dynamic, and for the loving family memories that might now be tinged with some darkness. But I was glad for her parents. They had found the courage to enter into the unknown in pursuit of their own happiness.

I met my husband—the man I would marry "for real," as I thought of it—at a Christmas party in Jackson, Mississippi. He was tall and lean and spoke with an easy manner, an endearing country lilt in his voice. On our second date, I scared him half to death when I confessed that I was married, but only technically. His eyes went wide and I saw the muscles in his jaw clench. When I explained that it was a green card marriage, that Antoine and I had broken up, lived in different states, and that I was simply keeping a promise I had made, he relaxed. "Could you not have thought of another way to start that conversation than 'I'm married'?" he later asked me. "I wanted to be honest," I told him. "I wanted you to know what you were getting into."

I remember the day my husband first told me he loved me. It was spring, and we were lying on my quilt, afternoon light filtering through the windows. Suddenly he flung his arm over his eyes, as though pained with a headache.

"What's wrong?" I asked.

"I want to tell you something, but I'm not sure I should," he said, his eyes still covered.

"Tell me," I said. "Now you *have* to tell me."

"But what if you don't want to hear it?"

"I promise I do." I lightly removed his arm from his face.

"Okay, fine," he paused, looking up at me. "I love you."

"I love you, too," I said. I didn't hesitate.

My husband's parents were never divorced, but they were also never married. He was raised by a loving mother and grandmother and has never had contact with his biological father. Social scientists have yet to study the marital outcomes of a child of divorce partnered with a child of a single mother. The future of our relationship is in uncharted waters, statistically speaking.

When my husband and I married on a hot October day in central Mississippi, my twice-divorced grandfather officiated the ceremony, and the four poles of our *chuppah* were supported by our respective mothers and stepfathers. Dad walked me down the aisle. "May your bond of love be as difficult to break as it would be to put back together these pieces of glass," Poppi pronounced before my husband stomped on the glass, shattering it to bits.

There is a certain amount of narcissistic faith required in any relationship, a belief in its superiority, a belief in yourself and the other person that, if closely examined, is absurd. Sometimes belief in the relationship feels religious, in that it can be mysterious and divine, or riddled with doubt. Ultimately, belief in love is a suspension of disbelief, like the creation of art. You have to believe in the art's extraordinariness, believe that what you are creating is unique and worthy of existing in the world. No one embarks on a marriage while contemplating its potential demise. Or at least no one admits that they do.

I never dreamed about getting married, about becoming a wife, the white dress I would wear. I wanted to write books, travel the world, speak another language fluently. As a teenager struggling to find myself, I had a vision that someday I would live alone in a seaside cottage with my daughter, partner-less and isolated, undisturbed. In my vision, the daughter was symbolic. I wanted to shelter and be sheltered. I wanted to be loved, to be known.

My husband and I are now expecting our first child, a girl. The vision I had for myself is no longer a symbol, but a reality rooted in doctor's visits and daycare waiting lists and my expanding body and swelling ankles. I think about the countless ways we will love our daughter, the ways we will undoubtedly scar her, the untold, unforeseen hurts and joys that are to come. I choose to believe it will be worth it in the end.

Now I understand that in order to be loved, you have to love, too. You have to risk the hurt that might come. You have to make small concessions and hope that the other person is also making their own small concessions (without ever knowing exactly what they are, because that would be cruel), and know that in the end these little losses will not only balance out, but you will have created something much greater than the sum total of your parts. Fairness is too small a word.

Epilogue

In the summer of 2020, as we accepted the reality of our isolation and moved all our gatherings, classes, and meetings online, my ex-stepmother changed her Instagram profile from private to public. Out of paranoia and masochistic curiosity, I had kept a Google alert on Krystal's name and periodically checked her social media. The Google alert had yielded nothing in the years since I had created it, and her social media posts had only been visible to her followers, not lurking ex-stepchildren like myself. But now, hundreds of her photos and videos were suddenly out in the open. In the years since we had cut our contact, Krystal had become a certified Zumba teacher. I watched snippets of the videos she posted from her makeshift basement studio. Dressed in neon and leopard-print athletic-wear, she gyrated her hips and pumped her arms to blaring reggaetón beats, punctuating her instructions with ululations and cries of "Yes, chica!" and "Sweat it out!"

For the first time in fifteen years, I heard her voice coming from my phone. I heard it with my whole body, the affectation with which she drew out her "a's," the overtly baby-ish high pitch she still used even though she was now in her sixties. In most ways, Krystal seemed unchanged from the last time I had seen her in person. Her hair was still long and dyed a brassy blonde, her skin still tan, though it now had the weathered look of someone who had spent too much time in tanning beds. She had clearly gotten the boob job she had always wanted, and likely some Botox, too. But the biggest change was that

Krystal no longer went by "Krystal." On Instagram, she had adopted a Spanish-sounding version of her name, more in line with the "bilingual" descriptor in her bio.

I told myself that considering there was a global pandemic, a little light internet stalking of my ex-stepmother was harmless. I even justified it as research for this book. I tried not to spend too much time with her digital presence, but I'll admit that on more than one occasion, I found myself glued to my phone, unaware of how much time had passed since I had decided to do a "quick check-in."

I found myself becoming a more frequent visitor to her page as the summer wore on. I knew to expect the highly filtered selfies she posted on Sundays with the caption "Sundays on the front porch." I found myself familiar with her front porch itself, which had a swing and flower pots filled with ferns and impatiens and a coffee table with a chic tray of candles arranged just so. I recognized certain pieces of antique mahogany furniture, certain still life oil paintings, certain coffee cups in photos she posted of her home. I recognized the gold crucifix around her neck.

Krystal was still the same Krystal. And yet, filtered through the internet, with her empty motivational catchphrases, her falsely affected mannerisms and Facetuned photos, she was so obviously performative it was laughable—"cringe," as the kids would say—that I wondered how I had ever been afraid of her. How had this small, strange, narcissistic woman terrorized me so? Was her presence a collective figment of my—and my family's—imagination?

My frequent visits to Krystal's Instagram page led me down rabbit holes, like finding the Facebook profile of her partner. From what I discerned, he had immigrated from Mexico decades earlier and had a career in landscaping. He tied his long, black hair in a ponytail, and he had a handsome face. He rarely posted to social media, and he seemed nice enough, but I wondered about him, wondered if he was maybe a little afraid of Krystal, too, wondered if he was the same man she had cheated on my father with. Did he know about us? Or were we simply skeletons in Krystal's closet?

Krystal had intermittently appeared in my dreams for years, but now those dreams were happening again with an alarming frequency due to my reacquaintance with the sound of her voice. Even more alarming was that sometimes in these dreams, I spoke to her like a friend. In one such dream, Krystal and I walked arm in arm through Park Meadows Mall, where I had hung out as a preteen, haunting the cheap jewelry racks of Claire's and sampling the Bath & Body Works lotions.

Eventually, I began to worry that Krystal would find out that I had been watching her Instagram videos, though I only visited her page via my gardening Instagram profile, which contained no photos of me or my family or even my name. Still, with a little bit of digging, she could easily trace the account back to me. How embarrassing that I was still obsessed with her. What would she say or do if she found out?

And so, I blocked her from all of my accounts. Internet Krystal merged once again with the Krystal of my memory, where she belonged.

I hope I've been fair to Krystal in this book, as I hope I have been fair to myself, and my dad, Sam, my mom and Cecil. There's that word again: "fair." Vivian Gornick says that "we must see the loneliness of the monster and the cunning of the innocent." Have I adequately captured Krystal's loneliness? I'm not sure. Sometimes I think I've been too kind. The truth is, I no longer feel haunted by her. In my day-to-day life in Mississippi, I think of her infrequently. I know that is true, too, of my family members. We still express relief that she is "gone," but the sweetness of that relief, along with the emotional intensity of those memories, has faded.

Up until the age of twenty, I found the idea of my mother and father—who, for years, could only communicate through a court-appointed mediator—being in the same room together without tension to be unthinkable. And yet that is what has happened.

When I was planning my wedding, my mother confessed that she had once dreaded the idea of Sam's and my future weddings. The prospect of having to share that day with my dad and Krystal had felt untenable. What a relief that she was gone now, that we could carry on as we wanted. On my actual wedding day, my mom, dad, and Cecil interacted amicably, comfortably. It was the first time that my relatives on my mom's and dad's sides had seen each other in decades, and it was—beautiful. The last traces of bitterness had dissipated with the years.

The perspective I'm lacking now is Krystal's—the woman I once considered my second mother, the woman who once pretended I was her biological child. Throughout the writing of this book, I considered the possibility of reaching out, of meeting with her, of asking the questions that have accumulated, then filling in the blanks. But that meeting would be about as helpful as falling down the rabbit hole of her Instagram page. That meeting will forever be relegated to my imagination. I know I wouldn't get the answers I'm searching for. I know some boundaries should never be breached.

Perhaps the strangest part of writing a memoir is in studying the pattern and play of memory itself. I find it unsettling the way mundane and beautiful things can remind me of the person who was cruelest to me. I still fold towels and underwear in perfect thirds the way Krystal taught me. I remember the names of the flowers she planted, flowers I still love, like hollyhocks and foxglove and cleome and four o' clocks and butterfly bush. I remember her elegant handwriting, her set of calligraphy pens. The scent of gardenia reminds me of Krystal, as does the music of Sadé and Norah Jones. Grapefruit spoons and asparagus ferns. Every Christmas, the oversweet aroma of paperwhite narcissus brings back memories of the bulbs she would force each winter in crystal dishes in the laundry room. Stovetop espresso makers and the movie *Moonstruck* starring Cher and Nicholas Cage. Cranberry-orange pull-apart rolls and banana bread with extra chocolate chips. Dixie Chicks songs, Mary-Kate and Ashley movies, Rachael Ray.

A secondhand sourness curdles these warm childhood associations. I remind myself that memory works in mysterious ways.

Flannery O'Connor said that "Anyone who survived childhood has enough material to write for the rest of his life." For me, this holds true, though these days I'm much more preoccupied with the present. The world of the child is so self-contained and self-referential, a dense jungle within a glass-domed terrarium, that no life experience will ever match its dreamlike intensity and sensory richness (except perhaps, that dreamlike period of caring for a newborn). Sometimes as I lie in bed, in the space between waking and sleeping, I walk through the rooms of each of my childhood homes—my mother's house on Lima Street, and my father's house on Jamaica Way. I allow them to be empty of people; only the things remain. I test myself to visualize the smallest of details: the dusty cool smell of the garage deep freezer, the distinct contents of each junk drawer, the color of the bathroom countertops, the sound of a C7 chord on the out-of-tune upright piano. These houses no longer exist as they once were in the physical world, and yet they'll live on inside of me until one day when they—and I—are gone.

Bibliography

Amato, P. R., & D. D. Deboer. "The Transmission of Marital Instability Across Generations: Relationship Skills or Commitment to Marriage?" *Journal of Marriage and Family*, 63, no. 4 (2001): 1038–1051.

Beckett, Samuel. *Molloy*. Grove Press, 1955.

Bettelheim, Bruno. *The Uses of Enchantment: The Meaning and Importance of Fairy Tales*. Vintage, 2010.

Calvino, Italo. *Six Memos for the Next Millennium*. Mariner Books, 2016.

Frank, Anne. *The Diary of a Young Girl*. Bantam, 1993 (reissue edition).

Goldenberg, David. "The Story Behind This Mystifying Photo of KKK Members at a Colorado Fair." *Atlas Obscura* (23 November 2015).

Gornick, Vivian. *The Situation and the Story: The Art of Personal Narrative*. Farrar, Straus, and Giroux, 2001.

Grimm, Jacob and Wilhelm. "Little Brother and Little Sister."

Strayed, Cheryl. *Wild: From Lost to Found on the Pacific Crest Trail*. Knopf: 2012.

Van der Kolk, Bessel. *The Body Keeps the Score: Brain, Mind, and Body in the Healing of Trauma*. Penguin, 2015.

Acknowledgments

Split the Baby would not exist without the help, encouragement, and recollections of many people.

Thank you to my fearless publisher, Belle Point Press, for lifting up Mid-South writers and expanding our understanding of what it means to make a home in this region. Casie Dodd, you transformed my manuscript into a beautiful book! I am filled with gratitude.

Split the Baby first came into existence as my MFA thesis at the Mississippi University of Women, with a terrible title that I won't mention here. I am forever grateful for the supportive faculty at The W, as well as my fellow cohort of talented writers. Thank you especially to Kendall Dunkelberg, Mary Miller, Brandy Wilson, and Ellen Ann Fentress for modeling how to be a generous reader, and how to write with precision and care. Mary, you believed in these essays before I did and opened doors for me. Ellen Ann, you showed me I could be a writer in the first place and offered me invaluable feedback as this book came to be. Thank you for all the pimento cheese sandwiches and for being a constant mentor and friend through the years.

In writing this book, I learned and drew inspiration from a wealth of writers including: Leslie Jamison, Esmé Wang, Kendra Allen, JoAnn Beard, James Baldwin, Chelsea Hodson, Kiese Laymon, Jesmyn Ward, Philip Lopate, Vivian Gornick, Dani Shapiro, Eudora Welty, Natasha Trethewey, and George Orwell. Adrienne Rich's essay "Split at the Root" showed me how to grapple authentically and honestly with questions of identity, and to engage in a lifelong practice of self-investigation and betterment. That essay is at the heart of this book's title.

Thank you to the Yiddish Book Center and their Tent Creative Writing Residency. My deep gratitude to Eileen Pollack for reading and offering feedback on the essay that would eventually grow into this book.

Thank you, Mississippi. I could not have written this book without your soil teaching me how to grow roots. Thank you to two dear Mississippi poets: Celeste Schueler for your generous spirit, and your letters and texts and poems, and C. T. Salazar for your solid advice and justice-oriented example. Thank you, Lee Durkee, for always showing up as your authentic self in life and writing, and for your support of my work. Thank you for the vital friendship: Liz Broussard (my Jackson ride-or-die), Claire Brown, Rebecca Rosencline, Mariel Parman, Meryl and Brooke Wilsner. Meryl, your writing and fearlessness continue to inspire me. Jan Hoover and Shannon Barbour, it's been a privilege to grow alongside you as writers since our fateful meeting in Ellen Ann's class in 2018. Thank you to Church Goin' Mule and JX Farms for providing me space to write in 2022. Thank you to Johnny and Deborah Wray for the refuge you've created at High Hope Farm and the Grateful House. Renee and Andréa Houston, thank you for the love you've shown me as your daughter-in-law. Thank you to the community of readers and writers at *Rooted Magazine* and to my friend and fellow editor Shira Muroff.

Thank you, Colorado, for teaching me how to find myself. Thank you, Kim, for sharing your memories and extending a hand across the years. Thank you, Les Katz, for writing the report that helped me see my childhood self and for generously meeting with me decades later. Thank you to my BFF Sarah Allexan. In sixth grade, we wore the same shoes and had the same crush, and we've never looked back since. Thank you, Suzanne Allexan and Steve Allexan for allowing your house to be my third home growing up.

My family was instrumental in the creation of this book. Thank you Poppi, Grandma Joan, Aunt Esther, and Aunt Hedy for being part of this story in important ways. Thank you Cecil, the best stepfather in the world, for always showing up when I need you, and for saving and sending and scanning so many documents that told the story of our family. Thank you, Mom, for always fighting for me, for being my number one supporter, for your fierce, unwavering love. Your voice is vital in this book and in my life. Thank you, Dad, for teaching me to always appreciate roadside geologic formations and for sending me sixty pounds' worth of family photos. I love you, and I'm so glad we've been able to learn and grow through hard and good times together. Thank you, Sam, for letting me tell this story, which is in so many ways your story, too. We're in this together, forever.

LaQuenza, thank you for your love and partnership, for cooking me delicious food, for always believing in me and for supporting every new project I dive into, whether it's selling kombucha at the farmers' market, or digging up chunks of our lawn to turn into flower beds, or writing a book. I love you now and always. Ava, I finished writing the first draft of this manuscript when you were still in my belly. Now that this book is in the world, I can't imagine a life without your exuberant, wondrous, joyous self. You will always be my greatest work of art.

"Mirror, Mirror on the Wall" first appeared in *Southwest Review* in summer 2020.

"Split the Baby" first appeared in *phoebe*, selected by Jami Attenberg in their 2022 nonfiction contest.

"Savior Complex" first appeared in *Harpur Palate* in summer 2023.

LAUREN RHOADES is a writer, editor, and grantmaker living in Jackson, Mississippi. Originally from Denver, Colorado, Lauren has served with AmeriCorps, started Mississippi's first fermentation company, and helmed the Eudora Welty House & Garden. She is now director of grants at the Mississippi Arts Commission and a host of MPB's *The Mississippi Arts Hour*. In 2022, Lauren founded *Rooted Magazine*, an online publication dedicated to telling unfiltered stories about what it means to call Mississippi home. She holds an MFA in creative writing from the Mississippi University for Women. *Split the Baby* is her first book.

Belle Point Press is a literary small press
along the Arkansas-Oklahoma border.
Our mission is simple: Stick around and read.
Learn more at bellepointpress.com.

BELLE
POINT
PRESS